A
LETTER
CONCERNING
TOLERATION

John Locke

A

LETTER

CONCERNING

Toleration :

Humbly Submitted, &c.

LICENSED, *Octob.* 3. 1689.

LONDON,
Printed for *Awnſham Churchill,* at the *Black
Swan* at *Amen-Corner.* 1689.

Edited and introduced by JAMES H. TULLY

HACKETT PUBLISHING COMPANY

JOHN LOCKE: 1632–1704

95 94 93 92 91   4 5 6 7 8 9 10

Cover design by Richard L. Listenberger
Interior design by James N. Rogers

For further information, please address
Hackett Publishing Company
P.O. Box 44937
Indianapolis, Indiana 46244-0937

Library of Congress Cataloging in Publication Data

Locke, John, 1632–1704.
    A letter concerning toleration.

    (HPC classics series)
    Translation of: Epistola de tolerantia.
    Bibliography: p.
    1. Toleration. I. Tully, James, 1946-
II. Title. III. Series.
BR1610.L823 1983   261.7′2   83–281
    ISBN 0–915145–60–X (pbk.)

The paper used in this publication meets the minimum requirements of American National Standard for Information Sciences—Permanence of Paper for Printed Library Materials, ANSI Z39.48-1984.

∞

To my mother and father

TABLE OF CONTENTS

Acknowledgements

I would like to thank the master and fellows of Nuffield College, Oxford, for electing me a visiting fellow and for their assistance during my period of research. I am also grateful to the librarians and assistants at the Locke Room and the Bodleian, Oxford, for all their kindness. The McGill University humanities research council has my gratitude for providing funds for much of my research. The Department of Rare Books and Special Collections, McGill University Libraries, has my gratitude for allowing use of the title page from the original edition. My special thanks go, once again, to Cathy Duggan for typing the manuscript with unparalleled skill and inexhaustible tolerance. Finally, for inspiration, let me acknowledge those who, from Locke to Bertrand Russell, Jacek Kuron and Noam Chomsky, keep not only the conversation but also the practice of toleration going.

Introduction

A Letter Concerning Toleration is a translation of the *Epistola de Tolerantia*, a letter written in Latin by John Locke to his close friend Philip von Limborch, a Dutch Arminian, during the winter months of 1685. At the time Locke was a political exile in Amsterdam, living underground in the home of Dr. Egbert Veen under an assumed name in order to elude extradition and persecution for his part in the revolutionary activity for toleration in England in 1679–83. The *Epistola de Tolerantia* was first published anonymously and without Locke's knowledge in May, 1689 in Gouda, after Locke had returned to England in the wake of William of Orange's conquest of the English throne in the winter of 1688. William Popple, a fellow radical whig and religious dissenter, translated the *Epistola de Tolerantia* into English, wrote a preface (included in this edition) and had it published by the whig publisher, Awnsham Churchill, anonymously, yet with Locke's knowledge, as *A Letter Concerning Toleration* in October 1689. A second corrected edition appeared in March, 1690. The *Letter* advocates toleration in the twofold religious and political sense of religious liberty and civil liberty, irrespective of the particular god one worships. This was far too radical for all but a tiny group of whigs who tried unsuccessfully to use the Convention Parliament to institutionalize the ideas of civil and religious liberty that had been developed during the Civil War and the early 1680s. The conservative religious settlement, encoded in the Toleration Act of May 27, 1689, denied freedom of worship to unorthodox dissenters (those who, like Locke and Popple, denied the Trinity) and Roman Catholics, and granted it—in the form of a revocable exemption from earlier anti-toleration legislation—to Protestant Trinitarian dissenters who took the oath of allegiance and obtained a licence to meet, but denied them access to public office. This rendered the dissenters second-class citizens, legally dividing the nation for 150 years until religious and civil liberty was established; but, by then the Anglican-dissent schism had fossilized into the permanent class division in English society.[1] The *Letter* was immediately attacked as being beyond the pale of reasonable or acceptable opinion, first as an atheistically disguised Jesuit plot to bring chaos and ruin to church and state so that popery could gain dominion, by Thomas Long, a staunch defender of Anglican hegemony, in *The Letter for Toleration decipher'd and the absurdity and impiety of an absolute Toleration demonstrated* (1689). Jonas Proast, the Chaplain of All Souls, Oxford, then attacked it and defended the establishment view that the govern-

---

1. See E.P. Thompson, *The Making of the English Working Class*, Middlesex, Penguin, 1968, especially chapter one.

1

ment has the right to use force (prosecution) to cause dissenters to reflect on the merits of Anglicanism, the True Religion, in *The Argument of The Letter Concerning Toleration Briefly Considered and Answered* (1690). Locke defended his views with *A Second Letter Concerning Toleration* (1690). Proast answered this with *The Third Letter Concerning Toleration* (1691), moving Locke to write *A Third Letter for Toleration to the author of the Third Letter Concerning Toleration* (1692), to which, in turn, Proast responded with *A Second Letter to the Author of the Three Letters for Toleration* (1703). Locke's reply, *A Fourth Letter for Toleration,* was cut short by his death in 1704 and the incomplete manuscript was published posthumously. Over the last fourteen years of his life Locke wrote over three hundred pages in uncompromising defense of *A Letter Concerning Toleration.*

The striking clarity of style and organization, the literary device of an interlocutor to state the anti-toleration or uniformist position and the superb translation by William Popple all help to make the *Letter* one of the easiest of Locke's texts to read. It requires no interpretation. However, not only was it written for an immensely well informed friend, it is also one of the most engaged of Locke's works; his reflection and judgement on the religious and political struggle in which he had been actively involved for thirty years. Therefore, in the first part of the introduction I have sought to sketch in the context of his arguments, to provide a tool with which to understand their point and reference and to delineate their genealogy. A brief discussion of toleration after Locke rounds off the introduction.

Although written in Holland in a period of debate on toleration, as well as of persecution of dissent by William of Orange, the *Letter* is clearly written about and in support of the dissenters' resistance to government imposition of Anglican uniformity and struggle for religious toleration, including civil equality, in Restoration England. The unstable configuration of power relations which constitutes this context was initially codified in 1660–62 with the restoration of the monarchy and national church. This followed a year of near anarchy in 1659 after the Protectorate, and before it the Commonwealth, had failed to transform the forces unleashed in the Civil War into a lasting form of politics. The Restoration settlement marked, first, the triumph of the Laudian clergy in the Anglican Church with their policy of rigid uniformity of religious worship, out-manoeuvring moderate Anglicans and eventually driving Presbyterians—who had struggled for a more comprehensive national church—into dissent. Second, the Anglican Royalist laity (Cavaliers) gained control of the Cavalier Parliament and passed a series of oppressive Corporation, Conventicle and Five Mile Acts, the Clarendon Code, to impose religious conformity on the nation and to surveil, isolate, fine, imprison and deport non-conformists. The Baptists, Independents, Presbyterians and Quakers who refused to conform, and so became known as non-conformists or dissenters, comprised about ten percent of the national population and were concentrated in urban centers and the western counties. The oppression of dissent was, as Locke and more recent commentators stress, brutal and malicious: fines through confiscation of goods often meant loss of one's livelihood and impoverishment; the thousands who were incarcerated in filthy jails faced beatings, sickness and often death.

The attempt to extirpate dissent failed, not only because the instruments of domination of the parish clergy and local magistrate were unequal to the task. For the first fifteen years of the Restoration the Monarch, Charles II, functioned as a counterforce to Anglican hegemony. As early as 1660 he declared 'a liberty to tender consciences' (toleration) and so his readiness to grant religious toleration as an indulgence provided it were enacted by Parliament; thus affirming his prerogative and recognizing his shared sovereignty. Parliament countered with the Act of Uniformity and other anti-toleration legislation, yet Charles II used his prerogative both to relieve the dissenters from persecution and to attempt—and to succeed briefly in 1672—to introduce toleration by Indulgence, and this partly because he desired to protect his fellow Catholics from persecution under the same legislation.

Given these tense power relations, which always seemed on the verge of recoiling into a situation of civil war—as in the uprisings of 1661 and 1663, the near rebellion and reaction of 1681–83 and the unsuccessful Monmouth Rebellion of 1685—it is not surprising that Locke understood religion, politics and political writing to be the continuation of war by other means: the battle for domination and interest by means of dissimulation in the unstable space between the Scylla of tyranny and the Charybdis of anarchy.[2] This way of analyzing politics and religion, which undergrids the arguments for toleration in the *Letter* and was no doubt reinforced graphically by the revocation of the Edict of Nantes in France and the execution and repression of dissenters after Monmouth's Rebellion in the summer of 1685, was first employed, *mutatis mutandis,* by Locke in 1659–1661 *against* toleration. In a letter to Henry Stubbe written in response to his defence of a policy of toleration for all religious groups (including Catholics) in 1659, entitled *An Essay in Defence of the Good Old Cause,* Locke used his calculus of domination, interest and stratagem to suggest that toleration was impracticable.[3] However, his first detailed analysis of toleration is contained in two tracts, unpublished until this century, written in the winters of 1660 and 1661 against two toleration tracts by Edward Bagshawe, *The Great Question Concerning Things Indifferent in Religious Worship* (1660) and *The Second Part of the Great Question. . . .* (1661). The great question was whether the civil magistrate has the right to determine and impose 'indifferent things' (forms of religious worship and belief not expressly stated in the Bible but standardly considered

2. John Locke, *Two Tracts on Government,* ed. and intro. by Philip Abrams, Cambridge, Cambridge University Press, 1967, pp. 118–119, 210.

3. 'Locke to S.H. [Henry Stubbe]', in E.S. De Beer (ed.), *The Correspondence of John Locke,* Oxford, at the Clarendon Press, 1976, vol. 1, pp. 109–112.

by one sect or another to be necessary to salvation). Bagshawe answered in the negative because in things indifferent everyone has the
right of private judgment, or conscience, which therefore sets the limit
to law.

Locke argued that the priesthood had cunningly perverted Christianity by introducing two false beliefs: that any variation in religious worship is a sin and that the sacred Christian duty is to correct deviation
and impose uniformity by force of arms. In fact, the true Christian
beliefs are that Christians should 'suffer one another to go to heaven
every one his own way' and that the Christian's only weapon is love
and persuasion, not force. These true beliefs, which are the premises
of the *Letter,* have been thoroughly displaced by the false ones and the
laity, deceived by this clerical stratagem, now believe it to be their duty
and their interest (worldly and heavenly reward) to wage holy war to
defend and impose their form of worship. Religious leaders thus use
religion as an instrument to stir the multitude to war and as a guise to
shield their ambition to control the state and exercise domination. Consequently Christianity has become 'a perpetual foundation of war and
contention', the enabling cause of 'havoc and desolation' and of the
spilling of 'the blood of some many millions' in Europe since the Reformation. Because belief change is not a rational process, arguments
about the truth and virtue of toleration—which are standardly advanced only by weak groups and only until they become powerful
enough to dominate others—will not dislodge the two firmly held false
beliefs. Since interest and duty are aligned this way among the multitude, and since the elites will use them to gain power, a policy of
toleration would precipitate a war of religious sects for control of the
state, just as it caused the Civil War and the disintegration of the state
in the 1650s. Locke therefore concluded that toleration was impracticable, an invitation to civil war, and would be practicable only if the
two beliefs ceased to be indubitable, intersubjective conventions,
thereby undermining the justification of the use of force, but he saw no
evidence for this until 1665.[4]

His solution was for every person to alienate irrevocably his or her
natural power, including over indifferent things, to an absolute
monarch, Charles II, who would then impose whatever indifferent
things he judged necessary for peace and the public interest, using only
custom and pragmatic considerations as his guide. This alienation
theory of absolutism was to change to the delegation theory of limited
constitutionalism and popular sovereignty of the *Two Treatises of Government* (c. 1680–82), to the non-alienation of one's sovereignty over
indifferent things in the *Letter* and to the justification of popular revolution in both. However, much of this early analysis was to remain.
First, the magistrate's power is secular in function: its object is solely
the public good (peace and security), not salvation nor even promotion
of true religion, and the magistrate intervenes in religious matters only

4. John Locke, *Two Tracts, op. cit.,* pp. 158–161, 211.

if they threaten the public good. His main objection to Bagshawe is that he posits the non-interference with the dictates of individual conscience as the rule for lawmaking rather than the public good. Second, Locke saw that the greatest threat to peace is a national church, which, being near the top, seeks to gain dominion and to turn the people against a non-compliant ruler. Locke advocated a non-sectarian absolutism: the ruler would relegate forms of religious life on the basis of unchallengeable judgements about peace and security, independent of and quite possibly in opposition to any, and especially a national church, 'which know not how to set bounds to their restless spirit if persecution not hang over their heads'. He even suggests that such a magistrate would be enlightened; would judge toleration of 'underling' sects the appropriate policy in certain circumstances.[5]

Thus Locke's analysis in the *Two Tracts* underwrites Charles' declaration of indulgence from Breda in April 1660 on purely pragmatic grounds, except that Locke envisaged an absolute monarch whereas Charles sought to share sovereignty in religious policy with Parliament. Unfortunately for the underling sects who might have been saved from persecution by Lockean enlightened absolutism, Charles, in exchange for essential financial support, was forced to share sovereignty with a parliament dominated by the national church, and so events unfolded exactly as Locke predicted.

Locke's next writing on toleration was to come in 1667 in four drafts of a thirteen page manuscript entitled *An Essay Concerning Toleration*. Clarendon had fallen from power, the Anglican clergy had disgraced themselves by fleeing plague-stricken London while the non-conforming ministers had gained widespread respect by remaining and consoling the sick and dying, imposition had divided not united the nation and so pamphleteering and political manoeuvering for and against Comprehension and toleration erupted. By this time Locke had seen toleration in practice in the Duchy of Cleves, based, according to him, on precisely those two beliefs he held to be part of true Christianity and essential to toleration.[6] He then became private secretary to Anthony Ashley Cooper, soon Lord Shaftesbury, a tolerationist since the Commonwealth and leader of the parliamentary and extra-parliamentary toleration forces until his exile and death in 1682. The manuscript is an arsenal of arguments to be used by Cooper to convince Charles II that it is both his duty and his interest to introduce toleration by royal prerogative. Locke made the case by dismantling some of the sovereignty he had given the monarch in the *Two Tracts;* not in order to give it to Parliament (which he never unconditionally trusted, even in the *Two Treatises*), but to return it directly to individual citizens, thus moving closer to the popular sovereignty of the *Two Treatises* and the *Letter*.

If the magistrate of the *Two Tracts* were to impose articles of faith or

---

5. *Ibid.*, pp. 124–126, 146, 169–170, 229–232.

6. 'Locke to the Hon. Robert Boyle, 12/22 December 1665', in *The Correspondence of John Locke, op. cit.*, pp. 227–229.

forms of worship that a subject believed not to be indifferent and to be untrue or unacceptable to God, he or she nonetheless would be obligated to obey the law because all one's natural liberty had been alienated to the sovereign. The subject would be guilty of neither sin nor hypocrisy because obedience to such a law requires the assent of the will alone and not of the completely independent faculty of judgement or conscience, the basis of belief. Thus the subject would not compromise his or her inner belief, which Locke conveniently took to be the essence of Christianity at this point. However, for the true believers in such a circumstance the olive branch in the form of a scholastic distinction between judgement and will, its wide promulgation by Anglican pamphleteers and very respectable Protestant lineage notwithstanding, must have appeared as simply the tribute vice pays to virtue. As the full force of the Clarendon Code was unleashed in the 1660s the majority of non-Anglicans rejected the conscience-will distinction between inner belief and outer behaviour, continued to believe that action must follow belief, defied the laws and suffered the punishment—immortalized in John Bunyan's *Grace Abounding to the Chief of Sinners* and *The Pilgrim's Progress*. For example, 15,000 Quakers—the most uncompromising of the non-conformists—suffered fines, imprisonment, transportation and 450 gave their lives; the experiential basis of the belief Locke expresses in the *Letter* and William Penn in *No Cross, No Crown* that suffering, not imposing persecution is the mark of the true Christian.

In the 1667 *Essay* Locke changed the beliefs expressed in the *Two Tracts* that no longer held up in the light of the evidence of dissenter behaviour. Now, if a person sincerely believes that an article of faith is true and a form of worship acceptable to God, and so necessary and not indifferent, then he or she evidentially will profess and act accordingly. And, because these beliefs are sincerely held to be necessary, they are necessary for the believer and therefore he or she must act in conformity with them to be saved. Consequently, to profess or act contrary to one's religious beliefs, even if the magistrate so orders, is a sin (hypocrisy) and destructive of one's supreme interest (salvation). This change in Locke's view of religious worship not only conforms to dissenters' behavior, it also explains and justifies their civil disobedience and damns compliance. The *Essay,* then, marks the transition to Locke's radically subjective view of religious worship in the *Letter*— 'that homage I pay to that God I ador in a way I judge acceptable to him'—which makes the individual, not the magistrate, judge of what is necessary and what indifferent.[7]

Toleration of conflicting beliefs and practices, then, is not based on the belief that these are a matter of indifference, as would have been the case in the *Two Tracts* or as some scholars believe is the case his-

---

7. John Locke, *An Essay Concerning Toleration*, MS Locke c28 (folio 21), p. 2, reprinted in Carlo Viano, *John Locke Scritti Editi e Inediti Sulla Tolleranza*, Taylor, Turin, 1961.

torically, but, rather, on the opposite belief: that one's beliefs are true and, with one's practices, are of infinite importance. Dissenter martyrdom apparently convinced Locke that individuals would hold onto their beliefs and practices in the face of authority, force and earthly self-interest. From now on Locke not unreasonably took this to be a fact about the post-Reformation individual and, as in the *Letter*, viewed attempts at uniformity as either wishful thinking or hypocrisy and the cause of revolt. Toleration is justified epistemologically in this, the most difficult of circumstances, not only because force cannot induce belief change but because, in an only seeming paradox, there are no known indubitable objective criteria for determining which beliefs are true beyond a narrow core of speculative and practical beliefs. This sceptical justification of toleration plays the major role in Locke's later Letters and grounds the inference that the virtue of toleration (and sincerity) must itself be part of the core, as he proclaims in the opening sentence of the *Letter*.

Whereas in the *Two Tracts* only belief was not alienated to the sovereign (because the individual has no power over it), in the *Essay* the individual retains as well sovereignty over the religious activity that he or she believes necessary to salvation. The function of the magistrate is, as in the *Two Tracts* and the *Letter*, to preserve the public good and so has the prerogative to prohibit religious opinions and activity only if he or she judges them to be detrimental to peace and security, not for religious reasons. Now, however, the subject is not obligated to obey a law prohibiting or prescribing what he or she sincerely believes to be a sin, but is obligated to suffer the punishment. This defence of passive resistance justifies the activity of the majority of non-conformists and disassociates toleration from the rebellions of 1661 and 1663, thus undermining the Establishment assertion that all dissenters are politically subversive and bent on a second Civil War. Locke then proceeds to argue that toleration is in the interest of peace and security. The hypothesis that plays a central role in the *Letter* and which Proast selected as his primary target is presented here for the first time: because force cannot change belief, imposition creates either hypocrites or enemies, unites all the sects into one hostile opposition and thereby causes what it is supposed to correct. Toleration removes the cause of hostility, creates trust and tends to cause the proliferation of sects, thereby dividing and weakening their potential threat to peace and security. The uniformists, of course, read the causal story the other way round.

Finally, Locke understood the Clarendon Code, and all anti-toleration legislation from 1667 onwards, as a clear case of a ruling group using the pretence of the public interest as a guise to legitimate domination of minority sects; and this, as with the exercise of power generally, to advance their interests. He then rounds the *Essay* off with two arguments which appeal directly to the self-interest of the rulers. First, his redescription of the 1662–1667 situation as one where the attempt to dominate under the ruse of either unity or conversion has caused disunity and increasing enmity, even atheism, and that toleration, latitude and persuasion may bring reconciliation, is also a claim that the powers-that-be are working directly against their long-term interest. This sort of appeal to self-interest was common in the pro-toleration literature but it had little effect. Those in power believed that dissent was subversive, were motivated by revenge for their mistreatment during the 1650s and their policy seemed to pay, in the light of confiscated goods and land, lucrative fines and the acquisition of offices. Locke's second argument was that God would punish extremely severely any ruler who engaged in dissimulation and dominion and thereby abused his or her trust. We can gauge just how much weight Locke thought this appeal to the ruler's interest in avoiding eternal damnation carried by comparing it with his reasons for not tolerating atheists and Catholics.

For Locke, as for almost all his contemporaries, only belief in a god who punishes the wicked and rewards the virtuous in an afterlife provides most individuals with the motive — self-interest — sufficient to cause them to act morally and legally. He had no doubt that an atheist, like a Christian, could have good reasons to act morally and legally, but if civil punishment or public approbation could be avoided, then only the overwhelming threat of punishment by an omniscient god could outweigh the worldly advantage of immoral and illegal activity. An atheist lacks the motivation to act socially and thus could not be tolerated according to almost everyone in the seventeenth century except Pierre Bayle. A Catholic, on the other hand, possesses the motivation but it is aligned with obedience, not to the social order but to the Pope. That is, a Catholic has an obligation to obey the Pope that overrides his or her obligation to secular authority and, as a result, has an overriding interest (eternal happiness) in disobedience if the Pope so enjoins. Thus Catholics could not be reliable citizens. Locke was willing to tolerate Catholics if they would relinquish their political obedience to the Pope but the various efforts for this failed. The fear that Charles II and James II would align with France and re-introduce Catholicism and absolutism fuelled anti-papal prejudice in this period, but the calculus of interest and duty, not prejudice, was the source of Locke's view.

The weakness of the tolerationists' power base was Charles' dependency on the Cavalier Parliament for money. They were forced to retreat in 1670 when Charles, short of funds, had to recall parliament. The Cavaliers immediately passed a Second Conventicle Act, increasing fines imposed on preachers and owners of meeting houses and agreeing to pay one-third of the fine to the informer. However, the movement achieved an important tactical victory and gained for the dissenters twelve months of respite and entrenchment when Charles issued a Declaration of Indulgence in 1672. In February 1673 Charles recalled Parliament again and both Houses united to force the withdrawal of Indulgence in March. The main justification put forward was that the Indulgence constituted an abuse of prerogative which usurped the coordinate sovereignty of parliament and introduced absolutism.

Cooper, now Lord Shaftesbury, and Locke, defended it as a legitimate exercise of prerogative for the public good even though it was against the law: precisely the sort of wide discretion Locke grants the executive (monarch) in the *Two Treatises*.

In June 1670 Charles, presumably seeking financial independence of Parliament, entered into the secret treaty of Dover with Louis XIV of France, agreeing, *inter alia,* to declare himself a Roman Catholic at an appropriate moment in exchange for money. Suspicion of this coupled with the Bishops' and clergy's cry of popery and the Cavalier charge of absolutism were sufficient to rekindle the popular fear of popery and absolute government and so disintegrate the Catholic-dissent-moderate Anglican alliance Charles sought to conciliate. In February 1675, perhaps as part of a strategy to recoup his losses, Charles issued an Order in Council to enforce the Penal laws against Catholics and dissenters in order to pacify the Anglican fears of Catholicism. Whatever his intention the effect was to precipitate a fundamental and irreversible realignment of forces.

In *A Letter from a Person of Quality to his Friend in the Country* (1675), a pamphlet standardly attributed to Locke in collaboration with Shaftesbury, Locke analyzed the new configuration of power relations in the following way. The Laudian party seized the favourable moment to endeavour to complete their fifteen year operation to gain ecclesiastical dominion in church and state, and this by freeing the monarchy from parliament, making it absolute and *jure divino,* yet subordinating it to the divine right of the church—'to set the mitre above the crown'.[8] Their power was to be consolidated by the introduction of a standing army. Thus, he saw the introduction of oaths of allegiance and to non-alteration of the present form of church and government in almost exactly the prescient terms of the *Two Tracts.* The countermove was the formation of a party (soon to be named the Whig party) led by Shaftesbury and composed of disaffected Anglicans, dissenters and a radical core of Civil War soldiers, levellers, republicans and commonwealthmen who had experienced religious and political liberty in the 1650s. The aim of this alliance was not only resistance but also to struggle to secure for the dissenters toleration in the twofold sense given in the *Letter* of religious and civil liberty, and apparently religious liberty for Catholics, first through parliament (1675–81), and then, when this failed, through armed resistance (1681–85).

This pamphlet marks the decisive step to the mature theory of justified armed resistance in the *Two Treatises* and the *Letter.* As in the *Essay,* beliefs which no longer conform to the facts are discarded. For obvious reasons the hypothesis that the threat of divine punishment is alone sufficient to constrain powerholders within the bounds of the public good is abandoned. What differentiates bounded monarchies from absolute and arbitrary ones is that not only do they have the fear

8. John Locke, *A Letter from a Person of Quality to a Friend in the Country,* in *The Works of John Locke,* London, 1823, vol. 10, p. 232.

of God but also the 'fear of human resistance to restrain them'. Therefore, as he explains, the threat of civil war is the defender of liberty.
Governments rule in accordance with the public interest only because
they fear the subjects' rightful armed revolution if they abuse their
power. Subjects, on the other hand, exercise armed resistance only
when governments act clearly against the public good because they fear
that they will not gain the support of the majority otherwise and that
the majority could crush their uprising. Therefore, the oath of non-
resistance and the standing army are instruments of absolutism because
the former would immobilize one side and the latter decisively augment
the other side of the tensely poised balance of force relations at the
base of the state, the fear of which makes politics, as the achievement
of the public good, possible. Locke, then, has moved back to his
analysis, in the *Two Tracts,* of post-Civil War politics as the play of
interests constrained by revolution on one side and tyranny on the
other, but now in support of armed resistance. The argument is worked
out with extraordinary clarity and intellectual precision in the *Two
Treatises* and *The Letter,* but the outline is already present. When men
are oppressed, as with the dissenters, they will resist, not only pas-
sively as in the *Essay,* but actively with force of arms, and they do so
'justly and rightly'.[9]

The 1675 pamphlet is a statement and, in fact, a fairly accurate representation of radical whig strategy: to use the threat of rebellion as
additional ammunition in their struggle to gain toleration through parliament. The moderate Anglican gentry-dissent alliance which constituted Shaftesbury's Whig party (an alliance which lasted 250 years)
won a majority of seats in the House of Commons in the three elections
for parliament from 1679 to 1681. In each parliament toleration bills
were introduced and then defeated, either by the Lords or by Charles'
dissolution of parliament. To break the church-monarchy coalition, ex-
posed in the 1675 pamphlet and confirmed by events, the Shaftes-
buryan Whigs introduced a bill in each parliament to exclude Charles'
Catholic brother James from succession to the throne and, although
this is not mentioned in the bill, to secure the succession of Charles'
illegitimate son, the Duke of Monmouth, who was Protestant and popular with the dissenters. If this plan had proved successful, monarch and
parliament could have worked together to enact and enforce toleration.
Although they failed in this, they succeeded in passing a bill of *habeas
corpus* and this has become the single most important legal resource for
the protection of dissent in the modern world. When Charles dissolved
the Oxford Parliament in May 1681, defeating the Whig's parliamentary
tactic, the moderate Whigs like Lord Halifax 'trimmed' and the radicals
turned to their other tactic: armed revolt. This too failed but not before
Locke wrote the classic whig justification of revolution, the *Two
Treatises of Government.* Shaftesbury escaped to Holland, where he
died, and Locke remained to become involved with Algernon Sydney

9. *Ibid.,* vol. 10, p. 222.

in the plot to assassinate the King in September 1683. Sydney was hanged and Locke managed to escape to Holland and became involved in the organization of the ill-fated Monmouth Rebellion of 1685.

The effect of the Whig strategy was to unite the opposition. Events persuaded the Cavaliers, now Tories, that non-conformity and whiggism were politically subversive and caused them to move to an ultra-royalist position, represented by their republication and use of Sir Robert Filmer's *Patriarcha*. Events convinced Charles that whigs and dissenters were regicides and commonwealthmen. The official reaction after 1681 was swift and brutal, unleashing the most severe persecution of the Restoration period. Ejection from public office and imprisonment of radical whigs, the mass hanging of 150 victims after the defeat of Monmouth's forces in 1685, executions and the burning of Elizabeth Gaunt, an innocent Baptist, at the stake effectively drove dissent, as a movement for religious and civil liberty, underground for 100 years. It also explains why very few non-conformists were willing to come forward when James II issued a Declaration of Indulgence in 1687 even though William Penn, the popular Quaker spokesperson, supported it. The reaction also decimated radical whiggism (apparently forever), creating a power vacuum that was filled by the respectable whig oligarchs who found themselves in power in 1689.

It is this battle for toleration and this persecution, this suffering and loss of friends, that Locke writes about in *A Letter Concerning Toleration,* with an intensity of moral conviction and of moral outrage unparalleled in western political theory. He now argues that toleration of religious and civil liberty is no longer a matter for debate or for the prudential judgements of the magistrate. It is necessarily, not circumstantially, a part of the public good, the denial of which constitutes both the cause and the justification of revolt. It is, as he says in the *Third Letter,* a *right,* embedding it in a tradition that would outlast his adversaries.[10]

As a result of countless battles of this kind from mid-sixteenth century France to the present, the collection of assumptions, arguments, terms, distinctions and justifications of toleration of dissent, of civil and religious liberty, many of which are Locke's, has come to be a fairly stable and traditional part of one of the two main western political and juridical discourses; that of the sovereign individual and his or her subjective rights. This collection was incorporated into the rights discourse — itself a product of the Ockhamist tradition in the fourteenth and fifteenth centuries — in the course of the revolutions and constitution-building in eighteenth-century France and the North American colonies, and of the long march for political and religious liberties in late-eighteenth and nineteenth centuries England. The rights discourse spread to Germany, was deployed in the liberal revolutions in Latin America in the nineteenth century and has been carried with col-

---

10. John Locke, *A Third Letter for Toleration,* in *The Works of John Locke,* London, 1823, vol. 6, p. 212.

onizers, missionaries, imperialists and revolutionaries to all countries of the world. Now it is the universal language in which disparate claims of oppression and aims of diverse resistances are articulated in a globally understandable form, from East Timor and El Salvador to Poland and Lebanon. The four major historical roles it has had partly account for its remarkable diffusion and persistence. First and primarily, the rights discourse since the fourteenth century, and including toleration since the seventeenth and eighteenth centuries has been used in strategies to challenge corporate sovereignty from below. It has functioned as an instrument to undercut the claims to privilege of a church or other corporate entity, separating church and state and justifying the active role of the male, and later female population in modern religion and politics. Second, looking at the first the other way round, it has served the modern state as a tool to disaggregate competing corporate claims to sovereignty and special status within its borders, constituting a civil society of legally and politically undifferentiated individuals. As a consequence of the fusion of civil and religious liberty with individual rights it has been historically connected with rights of private property, and thereby part of the stratagems in the nineteenth and twentieth centuries to protect private capital from the state and to disintegrate collective challenges from the working class and from nationalist resistance movements in the third world. (These last two groups soon learned to use it in their manoeuvres to gain their present positions.) Fourth, in the present countermoves by subjects constituted politically and legally in the course of these great movements, it is now turned against the concatenations of power it so recently seemed to serve in justification of forms of plebeian dissent in the northern hemisphere (nuclear disarmament, ecology, Charter 77, Solidarity, minority rights, etc.) and plebeian resistance in the third world.

In spite of its entrenchment in a discourse with worldwide moral force, as Amnesty International proves, the justification of religious and civil liberty has been politically and legally effective, so far, only in those countries that have built up, used or abused, *in the very course* of the struggle for toleration, appropriate legal and political institutions and practices: paradigmatically, parliament, law court and constitution. Civil and religious liberties have their foundations, not in their justifications seeming reasonable to us, but in their being woven into the daily activity of the courtroom and parliament over three hundred years (and this is why they seem reasonable). Even in countries where the rights discourse is firmly anchored in effective institutions, however, appeals to the toleration of dissent can fail because they are challenged and overridden by counterclaims. This is so because the rights discourse shares the halls of justice and the corridors of political power with, and is conceptually intertwined with, the other main western politico-legal discourse; that of the sovereign corporate entity (church, nation, state, culture) and its objective right. This discourse of right, which is a product of the revival of Roman law and the Thomist natural law tradition in the thirteenth and fourteenth centuries, has acquired and spread the counter-arguments to toleration. Dissent is subversive, religious and civil liberty are atomistic, disruptive of cultural identity, community or majority will, incompatible with national security and so on because there are objectively right norms of behaviour (natural laws, dictates of reason, traditions), for the community as a whole which ought to be imposed or orchestrated by the sovereign body (Pope, council, monarch, representative body, community itself, vanguard party, critical theorists). A number of Locke's points in the *Letter* are responses to classic arguments of this kind put forward by uniformists, especially by Bishop Stillingfleet in *The Mischief of Separation* (1680) and *The Unreasonableness of Separation* (1681).

Because the rights discourse has been the counterstroke to the dominance of sovereign right since the fourteenth century the two have spread together and become institutionally and conceptually intertwined. The discourse of right has been a resource to justify religious, nationalist and culturalist hegemony, to legitimate the surveillance and control of modern populations, to censor and suppress minorities and to defend national sovereignty. It can be, if I may put it this way, latitudinarian or comprehensive but not tolerant, and it cannot but oppress in the circumstances Locke isolated in 1667 as distinctive of post-Reformation individualism and thereby cause resistance.

On the other hand, in third world countries where those who now fight for these liberties have never been able to use the local political-juridical institutions (even though this is constitutionally guaranteed), where the struggle has always taken place elsewhere, then the appeal to the rights discourse is morally effective but practically ineffective; swept away by the compromised court, the police, the army, the torturer or the death squad. This can be partly explained by a Lockean analysis in the terms of balance of forces, interests and dissimulation. The local military, equipped with the latest in armaments and technology of population control, in alliance with powerful interests and legitimated by arguments from the discourse of right, effectively turns the threat of armed resistance into a pretext for repression. The military and the power relations of which it is a part, like the standing army in Locke's 1675 analysis, outweigh the threat of revolt and so perpetuate tyranny and preclude liberty. There are three countervailing forces working to establish a balance of forces. First, citizens in the countries that tolerate dissent can use their civil liberties to criticise their countries' economic and military complicity, thereby helping to realign interests and redress the imbalance of forces. Also, they can use their religious liberty to augment the assistance given to victims of human rights violations in the third world by church organizations; some of which, like the Friends Service Committees, date from the seventeenth century. Second, the United Nations has adopted the rights discourse as its official charter and has become a major force in disseminating and encouraging the institutionalisation of human rights. More recently the Catholic church has added its official voice to the global outcry against human rights violations and a large segment of the church, especially in Latin America, has moved to defend and extend human rights by working with and organizing resistance forces, such as the Christian base communities. Thus, after having produced these two forms of representation of political-juridical power, and after having embraced the discourse of sovereign right at the Council of Trent, the Catholic church now seems to be reclaiming its Ockhamist heritage. It is too early to assess the effects of the alignment of these two institutions with the rights discourse, both on the internal organization of the nation-states they challenge—and the universal rights discourse is a direct threat to the sovereignty of every nation-state—and on their own internal organization, but they will be of momentous importance.

However, Locke's analysis is deficient in a number of respects. First, even if there is a balance of forces, the threat of armed resistance is insufficient to establish these liberties (Locke's own case perhaps being an example), although it is often sufficient to maintain and extend them (England avoided a revolution in the nineteenth century partly because partial toleration was granted in 1689). Nor, needless to say, is successful revolution under this banner a guarantee of postrevolutionary practice. Several Latin American countries, for example, have constitutions which guarantee these liberties (El Salvador's constitution even contains the Lockean right to revolt), yet the constitution is nothing more than the non- or weakly institutionalized residue of an earlier revolution: the trace of its failed good intentions or its successful hypocrisy.

Third, religious and civil liberties, and individual rights in general, are, as we have seen with Locke, based upon an uniquely European representation of political power. That is, sovereign individuals naturally possess power, part of which (archetypally the power to kill) they delegate to government who exercise it through law in accordance with the public good, or else it devolves back to the people who then revolt (as in the *Two Treatises* and *Letter*). Individuals retain the other part of their power to have a say in politics and use the law (civil liberties), to speak to their god (religious liberty) or to engage in a range of private activities. This populist representation of power, always used against the more accurate descending, or alienation (as in the *Two Tracts*) representation of power in the discourse of right, is the product of European history from conciliar challenges to papal sovereignty to the English and French revolutions. It is not a particularly accurate description of modern political and legal power as Joseph Schumpeter and his followers have demonstrated. In addition, it fails to represent new forms of power that have appeared since the seventeenth century, involving the mechanization and normalization of life, which are not controlled by individuals, groups or government. These non-sovereign power relations have always been conceptualized, and so misrepresented, in the terms of the rights or sovereign right discourses, as when economic power is said to be held by a sovereign elite, or is exercised or delegated by individuals (in liberal theories) or is alienated by the workers and can be regained by revolution (in marxist theories). This illustrates the dominance of these two great discourses over modern social thought, but, in misrepresenting the power relations they generate analyses and forms of political action that are appropriate to a situation which does not exist. When Locke advocated civil liberty for dissenters he could be fairly confident that its exercise in court and parliament would protect them against religious domination because power resided there. However, in countries where the toleration of dissent is now recognized, the exercise of the political and legal mechanisms of dissent is relatively impotent against the anonymous configurations of power that dominate our lives today and threaten life itself—such as the military-industrial complex—precisely because these forms of power are not as our rights presuppose: neither the people nor the state is sovereign over them. The new forms of dissent emerging in opposition to these non-sovereign relations of power may mark the end of politics as we have known it since the seventeenth century, or, since they are expressed in the terms of rights, they may be incorporated into and strengthen the political-legal institutions.

If in many third world countries the struggle to institutionalize the rights discourse for the population as a whole is unsuccessful so far, it is not only because political power is historically centralist, replicating the sovereign right of the Spanish monarchy in Latin America, since this was the situation in Europe as well. It is rather that over the last 100 years this struggle has been deflected by the intrusion of webs of power that circulate through the modern state, the multinational corporation, the World Bank and the local military, elite and populace. It is a struggle in a situation of heteronomy to embody civil liberties and human rights in effective institutions and practices not primarily against, as in Europe, the political domination of the sovereign, but against completely heterogeneous forms of subjugation that work through foreign and local power centers. The limits of a Lockean analysis or an analysis in the terms of sovereign political power is illustrated by the impotence of Allende in Chile 'in power' in the situation of heteronomy.

This is not to say the struggle for civil liberties is useless today. On the contrary, they are the only bulwark, however fragile, against the brutalization of everyday life in many parts of the world. Since the rights discourse is now part of the normative culture of every country and is advanced by international institutions, the resistance to oppression will tend to take the form of a struggle for the establishment of liberty in its rights form. If there has been one historically decisive factor for success, it has been that the struggle for these liberties by the force of arms and the tactics of the battlefield has been carried right through into political and legal institutions and continued there by force of argument and political and legal tactics (with occasional reversals). The dissidents need to ground their liberties in political and legal activity to establish toleration, yet, in so doing, bind themselves to their word. (This scarcely happens unless they already practice what they preach in their own internal organization, as in dissenter congregations or in Christian base communities, Sandinista organizations and Solidarity today.) The opposition, defeated on the battlefield, can continue the struggle by exercising their civil liberties, yet, in so doing, they further entrench the practice of rights. To read the historical record this way is to recognize, as Locke did in 1660, that modern politics is the continuation of war by other means and, as he saw in 1667, that the only means that keeps it from converting back to war—in the form of either tyranny and repression or popular revolt—is toleration.

Further Reading

Locke's published works and manuscripts on toleration are listed in the bibliography. The most thorough study of Locke's thought as a whole and its relation to his political and religious activity, one which places toleration at the center of Locke's concerns, is Viano 1960. Ebbinghaus 1957 and Viano 1960 and 1961 offer solid analyses of the arguments and Kraynak 1980 advances a new interpretation. In addition to Viano only Cragg 1950 and Goldie 1983 discuss Locke's views in the light of contemporary pamphlets and political and religious activity. Abrams 1967 is an important account of Locke's early absolutism. Some of the intellectual background to Locke's alienation theory in the *Two Tracts* is available in Tuck 1979, and Franklin 1978 treats his mature theory of popular sovereignty in a sensitive manner. The constitutional issues involved, especially in the Declaration of Indulgence in 1672, are explained by Weston and Greenberg 1981. Locke's sceptical justification of toleration needs scholarly attention, but at least the foundations have been reconstructed by Popkin 1979, Van Leeuwen 1963 and Passmore 1978. The fear of divine punishment as a motive for obedience, which is central to Locke's argument on atheists and Catholics, is surveyed historically by Walker 1964 (one of the best books ever written on the seventeenth century). Wootton 1983 handles this theme very well with special reference to political theory, including Locke. Locke's religious and epistemological beliefs are set in the context by Yolton 1957 and his social beliefs by Hundert 1972. Solid surveys of Locke's political thought are presented by Dunn 1969 and Parry 1978. Locke's political activities during this period are described by Ashcraft 1980, Goldie 1980, Cranston 1957, Laslett 1970 and, as secretary to Shaftesbury, Haley 1968. For an important new introduction to Locke's thought and activity, see Dunn 1983. The composition, translation and publication of *Epistola de Tolerantia* are very carefully and convincingly reconstructed, and the best modernised Latin and English edition presented in Montuori 1963.

A recent general survey of the period is provided by Jones 1978 and a contemporary account by Burnet 1833. Watts 1978 is an excellent account of the dissenters and Lacey 1969 details their parliamentary manoeuvres. The classic analysis of the Restoration Settlement is by Bosher 1951. Miller 1973 covers the Catholics and Thomas 1962 and Cragg 1950 the major ecclesiastical events. Watts 1978 and Cragg 1957 discuss the persecution and Earle 1977 Monmouth's Rebellion, but the contemporary account by Calamy 1802 is essential reading.

Lecler 1960 and Kamen 1967 provide general histories of toleration whereas Stankiewicz 1960 surveys sixteenth and seventeenth centuries France and Jordan 1940 meticulously analyzes the arguments devel-

oped in England between 1603–1660. Apart from Cragg 1950 no detailed work on the pamphlet literature on toleration between 1660 and
1690 has been done, nor on the influence Dutch writings may have had.
Henriques 1961 traces the struggle for toleration from Locke to John
Stuart Mill. Watts 1978, Thompson 1968, Jacob 1981 and Lecky 1880 all
throw light on the diffusion of toleration and individual liberty after
Locke.

For the formation of the political-juridical discourses of sovereign
right and individual rights see Skinner 1978 and Tuck 1979. The fragility
of the toleration of dissent in the United States is illuminated by Donner 1981 and in Canada by Berger 1982. Power 1981 gives a picture of
the situation globally by discussing Amnesty International's role and
America's Watch Committee 1982 provides a well documented account
of the violation of civil liberties in one third-world country. Chomsky
and Herman 1979 and Lernoux 1982 present Lockean analyses of the
situation in the third world from a perspective firmly within the rights
discourse. For a view of South America from the centralist perspective
see Veliz 1981. A recent attempt to survey and adequately concep-
tualize global non-sovereign power relations is Barnet 1981. The point
that modern power relations are not as the rights discourse
presupposes them to be and thus the appeal to the political and legal
institutions of rights against them is inapposite, yet without alternative,
is discussed in an original and seminal way by Foucault 1980.

Note on the Text

The following text is a restoration of the first edition of William Popple's preface to and translation of Locke's *Epistola de Tolerantia* published in London in October 1689. It is this edition which Locke defended against the attack by Jonas Proast throughout the three further letters and never once questioned the accuracy of the translation. Once, in the second letter, he mentions a place where Popple uses words which 'very livelily represented' the author's sense. This edition has been collated with the second edition and the corrections in spelling and typographical errors made in the second edition have been incorporated into the text. Otherwise, the typically seventeenth century punctuation, capitalization and spelling have been retained. Approximately ten minor punctuation changes per page were made in the second edition, but these make no difference to the sense of the document and so have not been incorporated into this edition. It is, apart from the slightly revised edition by Montuori 1963, the only modern edition of the *Letter* in the form Locke accepted and defended.

TO THE READER

The Ensuing Letter concerning Toleration, *first Printed in* Latin *this very Year, in* Holland, *has already been Translated both into* Dutch *and* French. *So general and speedy an Approbation may therefore bespeak its favourable Reception in* England. *I think indeed there is no Nation under Heaven, in which so much has already been said upon that Subject, as Ours. But yet certainly there is no People that stand in more need of having something further both said and done amongst them, in this Point, than We do.*

Our Government has not only been partial in Matters of Religion; but those also who have suffered under that Partiality, and have therefore endeavoured by their Writings to vindicate their own Rights and Liberties, have for the most part done it upon narrow Principles, suited only to the Interests of their own Sects.

This narrowness of Spirit on all sides has undoubtedly been the principal Occasion of our Miseries and Confusions. But whatever have been the Occasion, it is now high time to seek for a thorow Cure. We have need of more generous Remedies than what have yet been made use of in our Distemper. It is neither Declarations of Indulgence, *nor* Acts of Comprehension, *such as have yet been practised or projected amongst us, that can do the Work. The first will but palliate, the second encrease our Evil.*

Absolute Liberty, Just and True Liberty, Equal and Impartial Liberty, is the thing that we stand in need of. Now tho this has indeed been much talked of, I doubt it has not been much understood; I am sure not at all practised, either by our Governours towards the People in general, or by any Dissenting Parties of the People towards one another.

I cannot therefore but hope that this Discourse, *which treats of that Subject, however briefly, yet more exactly than any we have yet seen, demonstrating both the Equitableness and Practicableness of the thing, will be esteemed highly seasonable, by all Men that have Souls large enough to prefer the true Interest of the Publick before that of a Party.*

It is for the use of such as are already so spirited, or to inspire that Spirit into those that are not, that I have Translated it into our Language. But the thing it self is so short, that it will not bear a longer Preface. I leave it therefore to the Consideration of my Countrymen, and heartily wish they make the use of it that it appears to be designed for.

A LETTER CONCERNING TOLERATION

Honoured Sir,

Since you are pleased to inquire what are my Thoughts about the mutual Toleration of Christians in their different Professions of Religion, I must needs answer you freely, That I esteem that Toleration to be the chief Characteristical Mark of the True Church. For whatsoever some People boast of the Antiquity of Places and Names, or of the Pomp of their Outward Worship; Others, of the Reformation of their Discipline; All, of the Orthodoxy of their Faith; (for every one is Orthodox to himself:) These things, and all others of this nature, are much rather Marks of Men striving for Power and Empire over one another, than of the Church of Christ. Let any one have never so true a Claim to all these things, yet if he be destitute of Charity, Meekness, and Good-will in general towards all Mankind, even to those that are not Christians, he is certainly yet short of being a true Christian himself. *The Kings of the Gentiles exercise Lordship over them,* said our Saviour to his Disciples, *but ye shall not be so.*[1] The Business of True Religion is quite another thing. It is not instituted in order to the erecting of an external Pomp, nor to the obtaining of Ecclesiastical Dominion, nor to the exercising of compulsive Force; but to the regulating of Mens Lives according to the Rules of Vertue and Piety. Whosoever will lift himself under the Banner of Christ, must in the first place, and above all things, make War upon his own Lusts and Vices. It is in vain for any Man to usurp the Name of Christian, without Holiness of Life, Purity of Manners, and Benignity and Meekness of Spirit. *Let every one that nameth the Name of Christ, depart from iniquity.*[2] *Thou, when thou art converted, strengthen thy Brethren,*[3] said our *Lord* to *Peter.* It would indeed be very hard for one that appears careless about his own Salvation, to persuade me that he were extreamly concern'd for mine. For it is impossible that those should sincerely and heartily apply themselves to make other People Christians, who have not really embraced the Christian Religion in their own Hearts. If the Gospel and the Apostles may be credited, no Man can be a Christian without *Charity,* and without *that Faith which works,* not by Force, but by *Love.* Now I appeal to the Consciences of those that persecute, torment, destroy, and kill other Men upon pretence of Religion, whether they do it out

1. Luke 22,25.

2. 2 Tim. 2. 19.

3. Luke 22. 32.

of Friendship and Kindness towards them, or no: And I shall then indeed, and not till then, believe they do so, when I shall see those fiery Zealots correcting, in the same manner, their Friends and familiar Acquaintance, for the manifest Sins they commit against the Precepts of the Gospel; when I shall see them prosecute with Fire and Sword the Members of their own Communion that are tainted with enormous Vices, and without Amendment are in danger of eternal Perdition; and when I shall see them thus express their Love and Desire of the Salvation of their Souls, by the infliction of Torments, and exercise of all manner of Cruelties. For if it be out of a Principle of Charity, as they pretend, and Love to Mens Souls, that they deprive them of their estates, maim them with corporal Punishments, starve and torment them in noisom Prisons, and in the end even take away their Lives; I say, if all this be done meerly to make Men Christians, and procure their Salvation, Why then do they suffer *Whoredom, Fraud, Malice, and such like enormities,* [4] which (according to the Apostle) manifestly rellish of Heathenish Corruption, to predominate so much and abound amongst their Flocks and People? These, and such like things, are certainly more contrary to the Glory of God, to the Purity of the Church, and to the Salvation of Souls, than any conscientious Dissent from Ecclesiastical Decisions, or Separation from Publick Worship, whilst accompanied with Innocency of Life. Why then does this burning Zeal for God, for the Church, and for the Salvation of Souls; burning, I say, literally, with Fire and Faggot; pass by those moral Vices and Wickednesses, without any Chastisement, which are acknowledged by all Men to be diametrically opposite to the Profession of Christianity; and bend all its Nerves either to the introducing of Ceremonies, or to the establishment of Opinions, which for the most part are about nice and intricate Matters, that exceed the Capacity of ordinary Understandings? Which of the Parties contending about these things is in the right, which of them is guilty of Schism or Heresie, whether those that domineer or those that suffer, will then at last be manifest, when the Cause of their Separation comes to be judged of. He certainly that follows Christ, embraces his Doctrine, and bears his Yoke, tho' he forsake both Father and Mother, separate from the Publick Assemblies and Ceremonies of his Country, or whomsoever, or whatsoever else he relinquishes, will not then be judged an Heretick.

Now, tho' the Divisions that are amongst Sects should be allowed to be never so obstructive of the Salvation of Souls, yet nevertheless *Adultery, Fornication, Uncleanness, Lasciviousness, Idolatry, and such like things, cannot be denied to be Works of the Flesh;* concerning which the Apostle has expressly declared, that *they who do them shall not inherit the Kingdom of God.* [5] Whosoever therefore is sincerely sollicitous about the Kingdom of God, and thinks it his Duty to endeavour the Enlargement of it amongst Men, ought to apply himself with no less

4. Rom. 1.

5. Gal. 5

care and industry to the rooting out of these Immoralities, than to the Extirpation of Sects. But if any one do otherwise, and whilst he is cruel and implacable towards those that differ from him in Opinion, he be indulgent to such Iniquities and Immoralities as are unbecoming the Name of a Christian, let such a one talk never so much of the Church, he plainly demonstrates by his Actions, that 'tis another Kingdom he aims at, and not the Advancement of the Kingdom of God.

That any Man should think fit to cause another Man whose Salvation he heartily desires, to expire in Torment and that even in an unconverted estate, would, I confess, seem very strange to me, and, I think, to any other also. But no body, surely, will ever believe that such a Carriage can proceed from Charity, Love, or Good-will. If any one maintain that Men ought to be compelled by Fire and Sword to profess certain Doctrines, and conform to this or that exteriour Worship, without any regard had unto their Morals; if any one endeavour to convert them that are Erroneous unto the Faith, by forcing them to profess things that they do not believe, and allowing them to practise things that the Gospel does not permit; it can not be doubted indeed but such a one is desirous to have a numerous Assembly joyned in the same Profession with himself; but that he principally intends by those men to compose a truly Christian Church, is altogether incredible. It is not therefore to be wondred at, if those do not really contend for the Advancement of the true Religion, and of the Church of Christ, make use of Arms that do not belong to the Christian Warfare. If, like the Captain of our Salvation, they sincerely desired the Good of Souls, they would tread in the Steps, and follow the perfect Example of that Prince of Peace, who sent out his Soldiers to the subduing of Nations, and gathering them into his Church, not armed with the Sword, or other Instruments of Force, but prepared with the Gospel of Peace, and with the Exemplary Holiness of their Conversation. This was his Method. Tho' if Infidels were to be converted by force, if those that are either blind or obstinate were to be drawn off from their Errors by Armed Soldiers, we know very well that it was much more easie for Him to do it with Armies of Heavenly Legions, than for any Son of the Church, how potent soever, with all his Dragoons.

The Toleration of those that differ from others in Matters of Religion, is so agreeable to the Gospel of Jesus Christ, and to the genuine Reason of Mankind, that it seems monstrous for Men to be so blind, as not to perceive the Necessity and Advantage of it, in so clear a Light. I will not here tax the Pride and Ambition of some, the Passion and uncharitable Zeal of others. These are Faults from which Humane Affairs can perhaps scarce ever be perfectly freed; but yet such as no body will bear the plain Imputation of, without covering them with some specious Colour; and so pretend to Commendation, whilst they are carried away by their own irregular Passions. But however, that some may not colour their Spirit of Persecution and unchristian Cruelty with a Pretence of Care of the Publick Weal, and Observation of the Laws; and that others, under pretence of Religion, may not seek Impunity for their Libertinism and Licentiousness; in a word, that none may impose either upon himself or others, by the Pretences of Loyalty and Obedience to the Prince, or of Tenderness and Sincerity in the Worship of God; I esteem it above all things necessary to distinguish exactly the Business of Civil Government from that of Religion, and to settle the just Bounds that lie between the one and the other. If this be not done, there can be no end put to the Controversies that will be always arising, between those that have, or at least pretend to have, on the one side, a Concernment for the Interest of Mens Souls, and on the other side, a Care of the Commonwealth.

The Commonwealth seems to me to be a Society of Men constituted only for the procuring, preserving, and advancing of their own *Civil Interests.*

Civil Interests I call Life, Liberty, Health, and Indolency of Body; and the Possession of outward things, such as Money, Lands, Houses, Furniture, and the like.

It is the Duty of the Civil Magistrate, by the impartial Execution of equal Laws, to secure unto all the People in general, and to every one of his Subjects in particular, the just Possession of these things belonging to this Life. If any one presume to violate the Laws of Publick Justice and Equity, established for the Preservation of those things, his Presumption is to be check'd by the fear of Punishment, consisting of the Deprivation or Diminution of those Civil Interests, or Goods, which otherwise he might and ought to enjoy. But seeing no Man does willingly suffer himself to be punished by the Deprivation of any part of his Goods, and much less of his Liberty or Life, therefore is the Magistrate armed with the Force and Strength of all his Subjects, in order to the punishment of those that violate any other Man's Rights.

Now that the whole Jurisdiction of the Magistrate reaches only to these Civil Concernments; and that all Civil Power, Right and Dominion, is bounded and confined to the only care of promoting these things; and that it neither can nor ought in any manner to be extended to the Salvation of Souls, these following Considerations seem unto me abundantly to demonstrate.

First, Because the Care of Souls is not committed to the Civil Magistrate, any more than to other Men. It is not committed unto him, I say, by God; because it appears not that God has ever given any such Authority to one Man over another, as to compell any one to his Religion. Nor can any such Power be vested in the Magistrate by the *consent of the People;* because no man can so far abandon the care of his own Salvation, as blindly to leave it to the choice of any other, whether Prince or Subject, to prescribe to him what Faith or Worship he shall embrace. For no Man can, if he would, conform his Faith to the Dictates of another. All the Life and Power of true Religion consists in the inward and full perswasion of the mind; and Faith is not Faith without believing. Whatever Profession we make, to whatever outward Worship we conform, if we are not fully satisfied in our own mind that the one is true, and the other well pleasing unto God, such Profession and such Practice, far from being any furtherance, are indeed great Obstacles to our Salvation. For in this manner, instead of expiating other Sins by the exercise of Religion, I say in offering thus unto God Almighty such a Worship as we esteem to be displeasing unto him, we add unto the number of our other sins, those also of Hypocrisie, and Contempt of his Divine Majesty.

In the second place. The care of Souls cannot belong to the Civil Magistrate, because his Power consists only in outward force; but true and saving Religion consists in the inward perswasion of the Mind, without which nothing can be acceptable to God. And such is the nature of the Understanding, that it cannot be compell'd to the belief of any thing by outward force. Confiscation of Estate, Imprisonment, Torments, nothing of that nature can have any such Efficacy as to make Men change the inward Judgment that they have framed of things.

It may indeed be alledged, that the Magistrate may make use of Arguments, and thereby draw the Heterodox into the way of Truth, and procure their Salvation. I grant it; but this is common to him with other Men. In teaching, instructing, and redressing the Erroneous by Reason, he may certainly do what becomes any good Man to do. Magistracy does not oblige him to put off either Humanity or Christianity. But it is one thing to perswade, another to command; one thing to press with Arguments, another with Penalties. This Civil Power alone has a right to do; to the other Good-will is Authority enough. Every Man has Commission to admonish, exhort, convince another of Error, and by reasoning to draw him into Truth: but to give Laws, receive Obedience, and compel with the Sword, belongs to none but the Magistrate. And upon this ground I affirm, that the Magistrate's Power extends not to the establishing of any Articles of Faith, or Forms of Worship, by the force of his Laws. For Laws are of no force at all without Penalties, and Penalties in this case are absolutely impertinent; becaue they are not proper to convince the mind. Neither the Profession of any Articles of Faith, nor the Conformity to any outward Form of Worship (as has already been said) can be available to the Salvation of Souls, unless the truth of the one, and the acceptableness of the other unto God, be thoroughly believed by those that so profess and practise. But Penalties are no ways capable to produce such Belief. It is only Light and Evidence that can work a change in Mens Opinions; which Light can in no manner proceed from corporal Sufferings, or any other outward Penalties.

In the third place. The care of the Salvation of Mens Souls cannot belong to the Magistrate; because, though the rigour of Laws and the force of Penalties were capable to convince and change Mens minds, yet would not that help at all to the Salvation of their Souls. For there being but one Truth, one way to Heaven; what Hopes is there that more Men would be led into it, if they had no Rule but the Religion of the Court, and were put under a necessity to quit the Light of their own Reason, and oppose the Dictates of their own Consciences, and blindly to resign up themselves to the Will of their Governors, and to the

Religion, which either Ignorance, Ambition, or Superstition had chanced to establish in the Countries where they were born? In the variety and contradiction of Opinions in Religion, wherein the Princes of the World are as much divided as in their Secular Interests, the narrow way would be much straitned; one Country alone would be in the right, and all the rest of the World put under an obligation of following their Princes in the ways that lead to Destruction; and that which heightens the absurdity, and very ill suits the Notion of a Deity, Men would owe their eternal Happiness or Misery to the places of their Nativity.

These considerations, to omit many others that might have been urged to the same purpose, seem unto me sufficient to conclude that all the Power of Civil Government relates only to Mens Civil Interests, is confined to the care of the things of this World, and hath nothing to do with the World to come.

Let us now consider what a Church is. A Church then I take to be a voluntary Society of Men, joining themselves together of their own accord, in order to the publick worshipping of God, in such a manner as they judge acceptable to him, and effectual to the Salvation of their Souls.

I say it is a free and voluntary Society. No body is born a member of any Church; otherwise the Religion of Parents would descend unto Children, by the same right of Inheritance as their Temporal Estates, and every one would hold his Faith by the same Tenure he does his Lands; than which nothing can be imagined more absurd. Thus therefore that matter stands. No Man by nature is bound unto any particular Church or Sect, but every one joins himself voluntarily to that Society in which he believes he has found that Profession and Worship which is truly acceptable to God. The hopes of Salvation, as it was the only cause of his entrance into that Communion, so it can be the only reason of his stay there. For if afterwards he discover any thing either erroneous in the Doctrine, or incongruous in the Worship of that Society to which he has join'd himself, Why should it not be as free for him to go out as it was to enter? No Member of a Religious Society can be tied with any other Bonds but what proceed from the certain expectation of eternal Life. A Chuch then is a Society of Members voluntarily uniting to this end.

It follows now that we consider what is the Power of this Church, and unto what Laws it is subject.

Forasmuch as no Society, how free soever, or upon whatsoever slight occasion instituted, (whether of Philosophers for Learning, of Merchants for Commerce, or of men of leisure for mutual Conversation and Discourse,) No Church or Company, I say, can in the least subsist and hold together, but will presently dissolve and break to pieces, unless it be regulated by some Laws, and the Members all consent to observe some Order. Place, and time of meeting must be agreed on; Rules for admitting and excluding Members must be establisht; Distinction of Officers, and putting things into a regular Course, and such like, cannot be omitted. But since the joyning together of several

Members into this Church-Society, as has already been demonstrated, is absolutely free and spontaneous, it necessarily follows, that the Right of making its Laws can belong to none but the Society it self, or at least (which is the same thing) to those whom the Society by common consent has authorized thereunto.

Some perhaps may object, that no such Society can be said to be a true Church, unless it have in it a Bishop, or Presbyter, with Ruling Authority derived from the very Apostles, and continued down unto the present times by an uninterrupted Succession.

To these I answer. *In the first place,* Let them shew me the Edict by which Christ has imposed that Law upon his Church. And let not any man think me impertinent if, in a thing of this consequence, I require that the Terms of that Edict be very express and positive. For the Promise he has made us, that *wheresoever two or three are gathered together in his Name, he will be in the midst of them,*[6] seems to imply the contrary. Whether such an Assembly want any thing necessary to a true Church, pray do you consider. Certain I am, that nothing can be there wanting unto the Salvation of Souls; Which is sufficient to our purpose.

Next, Pray observe how great have always been the Divisions amongst even those who lay so much stress upon the Divine Institution, and continued Succession of a certain Order of Rulers in the Church. Now their very Dissention unavoidably puts us upon a necessity of deliberating, and consequently allows a liberty of choosing that, which upon consideration, we prefer.

And in the last place, I consent that these men have a Ruler of their Church, established by such a long Series of Succession as they judge necessary; provided I may have liberty at the same time to join my self to that Society, in which I am perswaded those things are to be found which are necessary to the Salvation of my Soul. In this manner Ecclesiastical Liberty will be preserved on all sides, and no man will have a Legislator imposed upon him, but whom himself has chosen.

But since men are so sollicitous about the true Church, I would only ask them, here by the way, if it be not more agreeable to the Church of Christ, to make the Conditions of her Communion consist in such things, and such things only, as the Holy Spirit has in the Holy Scriptures declared, in express Words, to be necessary to Salvation; I ask, I say, whether this be not more agreeable to the Church of Christ, than for men to impose their own Inventions and Interpretations upon others, as if they were of Divine Authority, and to establish by Ecclesiastical Laws, as absoutely necessary to the Profession of Christianity, such things as the Holy Scriptures do either not mention, or at least not expressly command. Whosoever requires those things in order to Ecclesiastical Communion, which Christ does not require in order to Life Eternal, he may perhaps indeed constitute a Society accommodated to his own Opinion and his own Advantage, but how that can be called the Church of Christ, which is established upon Laws that are

6. Matth. 18.20.

not his, and which excludes such Persons from its Communion as he will one day receive into the Kingdom of Heaven, I understand not. But this being not a proper place to enquire into the marks of the true Church, I will only mind those that contend so earnestly for the Decrees of their own Society, and that cry out continually the Church, the Church, with as much noise, and perhaps upon the same Principle, as the *Ephesian* Silversmiths did for their *Diana;* this, I say, I desire to mind them of, That the Gospel frequently declares that the true Disciples of Christ must suffer Persecution; but that the Church of Christ should persecute others, and force others by Fire and Sword, to embrace her Faith and Doctrine, I could never yet find in any of the Books of the New Testament.

The End of a Religious Society (as has already been said) is the Publick Worship of God, and by means thereof the acquisition of Eternal Life. All Discipline ought therefore to tend to that End, and all Ecclesiastical Laws to be thereunto confined. Nothing ought, nor can be transacted in this Society, relating to the Possession of Civil and Worldly Goods. No Force is here to be made use of, upon any occasion whatsoever: For Force belongs wholly to the Civil Magistrate, and the Possession of all outward Goods is subject to his Jurisdiction.

But it may be asked, By what means then shall Ecclesiastical Laws be established, if they must be thus destitute of all Compulsive Power? I answer, They must be established by Means suitable to the Nature of such Things, whereof the external Profession and Observation, if not proceeding from a thorow Conviction and Approbation of the Mind, is altogether useless and unprofitable. The Arms by which the Members of this Society are to be kept within their Duty, are Exhortations, Admonitions, and Advices. If by these means the Offenders will not be reclaimed, and the Erroneous convinced, there remains nothing farther to be done, but that such stubborn and obstinate Persons, who give no ground to hope for their Reformation, should be cast out and separated from the Society. This is the last and utmost Force of Ecclesiastical Authority: No other Punishment can thereby be inflicted, than that, the Relation ceasing between the Body and the Member which is cut off, the Person so condemned ceases to be a Part of that Church.

These things being thus determined, let us inquire in the next place, how far the Duty of Toleration extends, and what is required from every one by it.

And first, I hold, That no Church is bound by the Duty of Toleration to retain any such Person in her Bosom, as, after Admonition, continues obstinately to offend against the Laws of the Society. For these being the Condition of Communion, and the Bond of the Society, if the Breach of them were permitted without any Animadversion, the Society would immediately be thereby dissolved. But nevertheless, in all such Cases care is to be taken that the Sentence of Excommunication, and the Execution thereof, carry with it no rough usage, of Word or Action, whereby the ejected Person may any wise be damnified in Body or Estate. For all Force (as has often been said) belongs only to the Magistrate, nor ought any private Persons, at any time, to use Force; unless it be in self-defence against unjust Violence. Excommunication neither does, nor can, deprive the excommunicated Person of any of those Civil Goods that he formerly possessed. All those things belong to the Civil Government, and are under the Magistrate's Protection. The whole Force of Excommunication consists only in this, that, the Resolution of the Society in that respect being declared, the Union that was between the Body and some Member comes thereby to be dissolved, and that Relation ceasing, the participation of some certain things, which the Society communicated to its Members, and unto which no Man has any Civil Right, comes also to cease. For there is no Civil Injury done unto the excommunicated Person, by the Church-Minister's refusing him that Bread and Wine, in the celebration of the Lord's Supper, which was not bought with his, but other mens Money.

Secondly, No private Person has any Right, in any manner, to prejudice another Person in his Civil Enjoyments, because he is of another Church or Religion. All the Rights and Franchises that belong to him as a Man, or as a Denison, are inviolably to be preserved to him. These are not the Business of Religion. No Violence nor Injury is to be offered him, whether he be Christian or Pagan. Nay, we must not content our selves with the narrow Measures of bare Justice: Charity, Bounty, and Liberality must be added to it. This the Gospel enjoyns, this Reason directs, and this that natural Fellowship we are born into requires of us. If any man err from the right way, it is his own misfortune, no injury to thee: Nor therefore art thou to punish him in the things of this Life, because thou supposest he will be miserable in that which is to come.

What I say concerning the mutual Toleration of private Persons differing from one another in Religion, I understand also of particular Churches; which stand as it were in the same Relation to each other as private Persons among themselves, nor has any one of them any manner of Jurisdiction over any other, no not even when the Civil Magistrate (as it sometimes happens) comes to be of this or the other Communion. For the Civil Government can give no new Right to the Church, nor the Church to the Civil Government. So that whether the Magistrate joyn himself to any Church, or separate from it, the Church remains always as it was before, a free and voluntary Society. It neither acquires the Power of the Sword by the Magistrate's coming to it, nor does it lose the Right of Instruction and Excommunication by his going from it. This is the fundamental and immutable Right of a spontaneous Society, that it has power to remove any of its Members who transgress the Rules of its Institution: But it cannot, by the accession of any new Members, acquire any Right of Jurisdiction over those that are not joined with it. And therefore Peace, Equity, and Friendship, are always mutually to be observed by particular Churches, in the same manner as by private Persons, without any pretence of Superiority or Jurisdiction over one another.

That the thing may be made yet clearer by an Example; Let us suppose two Churches, the one of *Arminians,* the other of *Calvinists,* residing in the City of *Constantinople.* Will any one say, that either of these Churches has Right to deprive the Members of the other of their Estates and Liberty, (as we see practised elsewhere) because of their differing from it in some Doctrines or Ceremonies; whilst the *Turks* in the mean while silently stand by, and laugh to see with what inhumane Cruelty Christians thus rage against Christians? But if one of these Churches hath this Power of treating the other ill, I ask which of them it is to whom that Power belongs, and by what Right? It will be answered, undoubtedly, That it is the Orthodox Church which has the Right of Authority over the Erroneous or Heretical. This is, in great and specious Words, to say just nothing at all. For every Church is Orthodox to it self; to others, Erroneous or Heretical. For whatsoever any Church believes, it believes to be true; and the contrary unto those things, it pronounces to be Error. So that the Controversie between these Churches about the Truth of their Doctrines, and the Purity of their Worship, is on both sides equal; nor is there any Judge, either at *Constantinople,* or elsewhere upon Earth, by whose Sentence it can be determined. The Decision of that Question belongs only to the Supream Judge of all men, to whom also alone belongs the Punishment of the Erroneous. In the mean while, let those men consider how hainously they sin, Who, adding Injustice, if not to their Error yet certainly to their Pride, do rashly and arrogantly take upon them to misuse the Servants of another Master, who are not at all accountable to them.

Nay, further: If it could be manifest which of these two dissenting Churches were in the right, there would not accrue thereby unto the Orthodox any Right of destroying the other. For Churches have neither any Jurisdiction in Worldly matters, nor are Fire and Sword any proper Instruments wherewith to convince mens minds of Error, and inform them of the Truth. Let us suppose, nevertheless, that the Civil Magistrate inclined to favour one of them, and to put his Sword into their Hands, that (by his Consent) they might chastise the Dissenters as they pleased. Will any man say, that any Right can be derived unto a Christian Church, over its Brethren, from a Turkish Emperor? An Infidel, who has himself no Authority to punish Christians for the Articles of their Faith, cannot confer such an Authority upon any Society of Christians, nor give unto them a Right which he has not himself. This would be the Case at *Constantinople.* And the Reason of the thing is the same in any Christian Kingdom. The Civil Power is the same in every place: nor can that Power, in the Hands of a Christian Prince, confer any greater Authority upon the Church, than in the Hands of a Heathen; which is to say, just none at all.

Nevertheless, it is worthy to be observed, and lamented, that the most violent of these Defenders of the Truth, the Opposers of Errors, the Exclaimers against Schism, do hardly ever let loose this their Zeal for God, with which they are so warmed and inflamed, unless where they have the Civil Magistrate on their side. But so soon as ever

Court-favour has given them the better end of the Staff, and they begin to feel themselves the stronger, then presently Peace and Charity are to be laid aside: Otherwise, they are religiously to be observed. Where they have not the Power to carry on Persecution, and to become Masters, there they desire to live upon fair Terms, and preach up Toleration. When they are not strengthned with the Civil Power, then they can bear most patiently, and unmovedly, the Contagion of Idolatry, Superstition, and Heresie, in their Neighbourhood; of which, in other Occasions, the Interest of Religion makes them to be extreamly apprehensive. They do not forwardly attack those Errors which are in fashion at Court, or are countenanced by the Government. Here they can be content to spare their Arguments: which yet (with their leave) is the only right Method of propagating Truth, which has no such way of prevailing, as when strong Arguments and good Reason, are joined with the softness of Civility and good Usage.

No body therefore, in fine, neither single Persons, nor Churches, nay, nor even Commonwealths, have any just Title to invade the Civil Rights and Worldly Goods of each other, upon pretence of Religion. Those that are of another Opinion, would do well to consider with themselves how pernicious a Seed of Discord and War, how powerful a provocation to endless Hatreds, Rapines, and Slaughters, they thereby furnish unto Mankind. No Peace and Security, no not so much as Common Friendship, can ever be established or preserved amongst Men, so long as this Opinion prevails, That *Dominion is founded in Grace,* and that Religion is to be propagated by force of Arms.

In the third place: Let us see what the Duty of Toleration requires from those who are distinguished from the rest of Mankind, (from the Laity, as they please to call us) by some Ecclesiastical Character, and Office; whether they be Bishops, Priests, Presbyters, Ministers, or however else dignified or distinguished. It is not my Business to inquire here into the Original of the Power or Dignity of the Clergy. This only I say, That Whence-soever their Authority be sprung, since it is Ecclesiastical, it ought to be confined within the Bounds of the Church, nor can it in any manner be extended to Civil Affairs; because the Church it self is a thing absolutely separate and distinct from the Commonwealth. The Boundaries on both sides are fixed and immovable. He jumbles Heaven and Earth together, the things most remote and opposite, who mixes these two Societies; which are in their Original, End, Business, and in every thing, perfectly distinct, and infinitely different from each other. No man therefore, with whatsoever Ecclesiastical Office he be dignified, can deprive another man that is not of his Church and Faith, either of Liberty, or of any part of his Worldly Goods, upon the account of that difference between them in Religion. For whatsoever is not lawful to the whole Church, cannot, by any Ecclesiastical Right, become lawful to any of its Members.

But this is not all. It is not enough that Ecclesiastical men abstain from Violence and Rapine, and all manner of Persecution. He that pretends to be a Successor of the Apostles, and takes upon him the Office of Teaching, is obliged also to admonish his Hearers of the Duties of Peace, and Good-will towards all men; as well towards the Erroneous as the Orthodox; towards those that differ from them in Faith and Worship, as well as towards those that agree with them therein: And he ought industriously to exhort all men, whether private Persons or Magistrates, (if any such there be in his Church) to Charity, Meekness, and Toleration; and diligently endeavour to allay and temper all that Heat, and unreasonable averseness of mind, which either any mans fiery Zeal for his own Sect, or the Craft of others, has kindled against Dissenters. I will not undertake to represent how happy and how great would be the Fruit, both in Church and State, if the Pulpits every where founded with this Doctrine of Peace and Toleration; lest I should seem to reflect too severely upon those Men whose Dignity I desire not to detract from, nor would have it diminished either by others or themselves. But this I say, That thus it ought to be. And if any one that professes himself to be a Minister of the Word of God, a Preacher of the Gospel of Peace, teach otherwise, he either understands not, or neglects the Business of his Calling, and shall one day give account thereof unto the Prince of Peace. If Christians are to be admonished that they abstain from all manner of Revenge, even after repeated Provocations and multiplied Injuries, how much more ought they who suffer nothing, who have had no harm done them, forbear Violence, and abstain from all manner of ill usage towards those from whom they have received none. This Caution and Temper they ought certainly to use towards those who mind only their own Business, and are sollicitous for nothing but that (whatever Men think of them) they may worship God in that manner which they are persuaded is acceptable to him, and in which they have the strongest hopes of Eternal Salvation. In private domestick Affairs, in the management of Estates, in the conservation of Bodily Health, every man may consider what suits his own conveniency, and follow what course he likes best. No man complains of the ill management of his Neighbour's Affairs. No man is angry with another for an Error committed in sowing his Land, or in marrying his Daughter. No body corrects a Spendthrift for consuming his Substance in Taverns. Let any man pull down, or build, or make whatsoever Expences he pleases, no body murmurs, no body controuls him; he has his Liberty. But if any man do not frequent the Church, if he do not there conform his Behaviour exactly to the accustomed Ceremonies, or if he brings not his Children to be initiated in the Sacred Mysteries of this or the other Congregation; this immediately causes an Uproar. The Neighbourhood is filled with Noise and Clamour. Every one is ready to be the Avenger of so great a Crime. And the Zealots hardly have the patience to refrain from Violence and Rapine, so long till the Cause be heard, and the poor man be, according to Form, condemned to the loss of Liberty, Goods, or Life. Oh that our Ecclesiastical Orators, of every Sect, would apply themselves with all the strength of Arguments that they are able, to the confounding of mens Errors! But let them spare their Persons. Let them not supply their want of Reasons with the Instruments of Force, which belong to another Jurisdiction, and do ill become a Churchman's Hands. Let them not call in the Magistrate's Authority to the aid of their Eloquence, or Learning; lest, perhaps, whilst they pretend only Love for the Truth, this their intemperate Zeal, breathing nothing but Fire and Sword, betray their Ambition, and shew that what they desire is Temporal Dominion. For it will be very difficult to persuade men of Sense, that he, who with dry Eyes, and satisfaction of mind, can deliver his Brother unto the Executioner, to be burnt alive, does sincerely and heartily concern himself to save that Brother from the Flames of Hell in the World to come.

In the last place. Let us now consider what is the Magistrate's Duty in the Business of Toleration: which certainly is very considerable.

We have already proved, That the Care of Souls does not belong to the Magistrate: Not a Magisterial Care, I mean, (if I may so call it) which consists in prescribing by Laws, and compelling by Punishments. But a charitable Care, which consists in teaching, admonishing, and persuading, cannot be denied unto any man. The Care therefore of every man's Soul belongs unto himself, and is to be left unto himself. But what if he neglect the Care of his Soul? I answer, What if he neglect the Care of his Health, or of his Estate, which things are nearlier related to the Government of the Magistrate than the other? Will the Magistrate provide by an express Law, That such an one shall not become poor or sick? Laws provide, as much as is possible, that the Goods and Health of Subjects be not injured by the Fraud or Violence of others; they do not guard them from the Negligence or Ill-husbandry of the Possessors themselves. No man can be forced to be Rich or Healthful, whether he will or no. Nay, God himself will not save men against their wills. Let us suppose, however, that some Prince were desirous to force his Subjects to accumulate Riches, or to preserve the Health and Strength of their Bodies. Shall it be provided by Law, that they must consult none but *Roman* Physicians, and shall every one be bound to live according to their Prescriptions? What, shall no Potion, no Broth, be taken, but what is prepared either in the *Vatican,* suppose, or in a *Geneva* Shop? Or, to make these Subjects rich, shall they all be obliged by Law to become Merchants, or Musicians? Or, shall every one turn Victualler, or Smith, because there are some that maintain their Families plentifully, and grow rich in those Professions? But it may be said, There are a thousand ways to Wealth, but one only way to Heaven. 'Tis well said indeed, especially by those that plead for compelling men into this or the other Way. For if there were several ways that lead thither, there would not be so much as a pretence left for Compulsion. But now if I be marching on with my utmost Vigour, in that way which, according to the Sacred Geography, leads straight to *Jerusalem;* Why am I beaten and ill used by others, because, perhaps, I wear not Buskins; because my Hair is not of the right Cut; because perhaps I have not been dip't in the right Fashion; because I eat Flesh upon the Road, or some other Food which agrees with my Stomach; because I avoid certain Byways, which seem unto me to lead into

Briars or Precipices; because amongst the several Paths that are in the same Road, I choose that to walk in which seems to be the straightest and cleanest; because I avoid to keep company with some Travellers that are less grave, and others that are more sowre than they ought to be; or in fine, because I follow a Guide that either is, or is not, clothed in White, and crowned with a Miter? Certainly, if we consider right, we shall find that for the most part they are such frivolous things as these, that (without any prejudice to Religion or the Salvation of Souls, if not accompanied with Superstition or Hypocrisie) might either be observed or omitted; I say they are such like things as these, which breed implacable Enmities amongst Christian Brethren, who are all agreed in the Substantial and truly Fundamental part of Religion.

But let us grant unto these Zealots, who condemn all things that are not of their Mode, that from these Circumstances arise different Ends. What shall we conclude from thence? There is only one of these which is the true way to Eternal Happiness. But in this great variety of ways that men follow, it is still doubted which is this right one. Now neither the care of the Commonwealth, nor the right of enacting Laws, does discover this way that leads to Heaven more certainly to the Magistrate, than every private mans Search and Study discovers it unto himself. I have a weak Body, sunk under a languishing Disease, for which (I suppose) there is one only Remedy, but that unknown. Does it therefore belong unto the Magistrate to prescribe me a Remedy, because there is but one, and because it is unknown? Because there is but one way for me to escape Death, will it therefore be safe for me to do whatsoever the Magistrate ordains? Those things that every man ought sincerely to enquire into himself, and by Meditation, Study, Search, and his own Endeavours, attain the Knowledge of, cannot be looked upon as the Peculiar Possession of any one sort of Men. Princes indeed are born Superior unto other men in Power, but in Nature equal. Neither the Right, nor the Art of Ruling, does necessarily carry along with it the certain Knoweldge of other things; and least of all of the true Religion. For if it were so, how could it come to pass that the Lords of the Earth should differ so vastly as they do in Religious Matters? But let us grant that it is probable the way to Eternal Life may be better known by a Prince than by his Subjects; or at least, that in this incertitude of things, the safest and most commodious way for private Persons is to follow his Dictates. You will say, what then? If he should bid you follow Merchandise for your Livelihood, would you decline that Course for fear it should not succeed? I answer: I would turn Merchant upon the Princes command, because in case I should have ill Success in Trade, he is abundantly able to make up my Loss some other way. If it be true, as he pretends, that he desires I should thrive and grow rich, he can set me up again when unsuccessful Voyages have broke me. But this is not the Case, in the things that regard the Life to come. If there I take a wrong Course, if in that respect I am once undone, it is not in the Magistrates Power to repair my Loss, to ease my Suffering, nor to restore me in any measure, much less entirely, to a good Estate. What Security can be given for the Kingdom of Heaven?

Perhaps some will say that they do not suppose this infallible Judgment, that all men are bound to follow in the Affairs of Religion, to be in the Civil Magistrate, but in the Church. What the Church has determined, that the Civil Magistrate orders to be observed; and he provides by his Authority that no body shall either act or believe, in the business of Religion, otherwise than the Church teaches. So that the Judgment of those things is in the Church. The Magistrate himself yields Obedience thereunto, and requires the like Obedience from others. I answer: Who sees not how frequently the Name of the Church, which was so venerable in the time of the Apostles, has been made use of to throw Dust in Peoples Eyes, in following Ages? But however, in the present case it helps us not. The one only narrow way which leads to Heaven is not better known to the Magistrate than to private Persons, and therefore I cannot safely take him for my Guide, who may probably be as ignorant of the way as my self, and who certainly is less concerned for my Salvation than I my self am. Amongst so many Kings of the *Jews,* how many of them were there whom any *Israelite,* thus blindly following, had not fall'n into Idolatry, and thereby into Destruction? Yet nevertheless, you bid me be of good Courage, and tell me that all is now safe and secure, because the Magistrate does not now enjoin the observance of his own Decrees in matters of Religion, but only the Decrees of the Church. Of what Church I beseech you? Of that certainly which likes him best. As if he that compels me by Laws and Penalties to enter into this or the other Church, did not interpose his own Judgment in the matter. What difference is there whether he lead me himself, or deliver me over to be led by others? I depend both ways upon his Will, and it is he that determines both ways of my eternal State. Would an *Israelite,* that had worshipped *Baal* upon the Command of his King, have been in any better condition, because some body had told him that the King ordered nothing in Religion upon his own Head, nor commanded any thing to be done by his Subjects in Divine Worship, but what was approved by the Counsel of Priests, and declared to be of Divine Right by the Doctors of their Church? If the Religion of any Church become therefore true and saving, because the Head of that Sect, the Prelates and Priests, and those of that Tribe, do all of them, with all their might, extol and praise it; what Religion can ever be accounted erroneous, false and destructive? I am doubtful concerning the Doctrine of the *Socinians,* I am suspicious of the way of Worship practised by the *Papists,* or *Lutherans;* will it be ever a jot the safer for me to join either unto the one or the other of those Churches, upon the Magistrates Command, because he commands nothing in Religion but by the Authority and Counsel of the Doctors of that Church?

But to speak the truth, we must acknowledge that the Church (if a Convention of Clergy-men, making Canons, must be called by that Name) is for the most part more apt to be influenced by the Court, than the Court by the Church. How the Church was under the Vicissitude of Orthodox and Arrian Emperors is very well known. Or if those things be too remote, our modern *English* History affords us fresh Examples, in the Reigns of *Henry* the *8th, Edward* the *6th, Mary,* and *Elizabeth,* how easily and smoothly the Clergy changed their Decrees, their Articles of Faith, their Form of Worship, everything, according to the inclination of those Kings and Queens. Yet were those Kings and Queens of such different minds, in point of Religion, and enjoined thereupon such different things, that no man in his Wits (I had almost said none but an Atheist) will presume to say that any sincere and upright Worshipper of God could, with a safe Conscience, obey their several Decrees. To conclude. It is the same thing whether a King that prescribes Laws to another mans Religion pretend to do it by his own Judgment, or by the Ecclesiastical Authority and Advice of others. The Decisions of Church-men, whose Differences and Disputes are sufficiently known, cannot be any sounder, or safer than his: Nor can all their Suffrages joined together add any new strength unto the Civil Power. Tho this also must be taken notice of, that Princes seldom have any regard to the Suffrages of Ecclesiasticks that are not Favourers of their own Faith and way of Worship.

But after all, the *principal Consideration,* and which absolutely determines this Controversie, is this. Although the Magistrates Opinion in Religion be sound, and the way that he appoints be truly Evangelical, yet if I be not thoroughly perswaded thereof in my own mind, there will be no safety for me in following it. No way whatsoever that I shall walk in, against the Dictates of my Conscience, will ever bring me to the Mansions of the Blessed. I may grow rich by an Art that I take not delight in; I may be cured of some Disease by Remedies that I have not Faith in; but I cannot be saved by a Religion that I distrust, and by a Worship that I abhor. It is in vain for an Unbeliever to take up the outward shew of another mans Profession. Faith only, and inward Sincerity, are the things that procure acceptance with God. The most likely and most approved Remedy can have no effect upon the Patient, if his Stomach reject it as soon taken. And you will in vain cram a Medicine down a sick mans Throat, which his particular Constitution will be sure to turn into Poison. In a word. Whatsoever may be doubtful in Religion, yet this at least is certain, that no Religion, which I believe not to be true, can be either true, or profitable unto me. In vain therefore do Princes compel their Subjects to come into their Church-communion, under pretence of saving their Souls. If they believe, they will come of their own accord; if they believe not, their coming will nothing avail them. How great soever, in fine, may be the pretence of Good-will, and Charity, and concern for the Salvation of mens Souls, men cannot be forced to be saved whether they will or no. And therefore, when all is done, they must be left to their own Consciences.

Having thus at length freed men from all Dominion over one another in matters of Religion, let us now consider what they are to do. All men know and acknowledge that God ought to be publickly worshipped. Why otherwise do they compel one another unto the publick Assemblies? Men therefore constituted in this liberty are to enter into some Religious Society, that they may meet together, not only for mutual Edification, but to own to the world that they worship God, and offer unto his divine Majesty such service as they themselves are not ashamed of, and such as they think not unworthy of him, nor unacceptable to him; and finally that by the purity of Doctrine, Holiness of Life, and Decent form of Worship, they may draw others unto the love of the true Religion, and perform such other things in Religion as cannot be done by each private man apart.

These Religious Societies I call Churches: and these I say the Magistrate ought to tolerate. For the business of these Assemblies of the People is nothing but what is lawful for every man in particular to take care of; I mean the Salvation of their Souls: nor in this case is there any difference between the National Church, and other separated Congregations.

But as in every Church there are two things especially to be considered; The outward Form and Rites of Worship, And the Doctrines and Articles of Faith; these things must be handled each distinctly; that so the whole matter of Toleration may the more clearly be understood.

Concerning outward Worship, I say (in the first place) that the Magistrate has no Power to enforce by Law, either in his own Church, or much less in another, the use of any Rites or Ceremonies whatsoever in the Worship of God. And this, not only because these Churches are free Societies, but because whatsoever is practised in the Worship of God, is only so far justifiable as it is believed by those that practise it to be acceptable unto him. Whatsoever is not done with that assurance of Faith, is neither well in it self, nor can it be acceptable to God. To impose such things therefore upon any People, contrary to their own Judgment, is in effect to command them to offend God; which, considering that the end of all Religion is to please him, and that Liberty is essentially necessary to that End, appears to be absurd beyond expression.

But perhaps it may be concluded from hence, that I deny unto the Magistrate all manner of Power about indifferent things; which if it be not granted, the whole Subject-matter of Law-making is taken away. No, I readily grant that Indifferent Things, and perhaps none but such, are subjected to the Legislative Power. But it does not therefore follow, that the Magistrate may ordain whatsoever he pleases concerning any thing that is indifferent. The Publick Good is the Rule and Measure of all Law-making. If a thing be not useful to the Commonwelath, tho' it be never so indifferent, it may not presently be established by Law.

And further: Things never so indifferent in their own nature, when they are brought into the Church and Worship of God, are removed out of the reach of the Magistrate's Jurisdiction; because in that use they have no connection at all with Civil Affairs. The only business of the Church is the Salvation of Souls: and it no ways concerns the Common-wealth, or any Member of it, that this, or the other Ceremony be there made use of. Neither the Use, nor the Omission of any Ceremonies, in those Religious Assemblies, does either advantage or prejudice the Life, Liberty, or Estate of any man. For Example: Let it be granted, that the washing of an Infant with water is in it self an indifferent thing. Let it be granted also, that if the Magistrate understand such washing to be profitable to the curing or preventing of any Disease that Children are subject unto, and esteem the matter weighty enough to be taken care of by a Law, in that case he may order it to be done. But will any one therefore say, that a Magistrate has the same Right to ordain, by Law, that all Children shall be baptized by Priests, in the sacred Font, in order to the purification of their Souls? The extream difference of these two Cases is visible to every one at first sight. Or let us apply the last Case to the Child of a *Jew,* and the things speaks it self. For what hinders but a Christian Magistrate may have Subjects that are *Jews?* Now if we acknowledge that such an Inquiry may not be done unto a *Jew,* as to compel him, against his own Opinion, to practice in his Religion a thing that is in its nature indifferent; how can we maintain that any thing of this kind may be done to a Christian?

Again: Things in their own nature indifferent cannot, by any human Authority, be made any part of the Worship of God; for this very reason; because they are indifferent. For since indifferent things are not capable, by any Virtue of their own, to propitiate the Deity; no human Power or Authority can confer on them so much Dignity and Excellency as to enable them to do it. In the common Affairs of Life, that use of indifferent things which God has not forbidden, is free and lawful: and therefore in those things human Authority has place. But it is not so in matters of Religion. Things indifferent are not otherwise lawful in the Worship of God than as they are instituted by God himself; and as he, by some positive command, has ordain'd them to be made a part of that Worship which he will vouchsafe to accept of at the hands of poor sinful men. Nor when an incensed Deity shall ask us, *Who has required these, or such like things at our hands?* will it be enough to answer him, that the Magistrate commanded them. If civil Jurisdiction extended thus far, what might not lawfully be introduced into Religion? What hodge-podge of Ceremonies, what superstitious Inventions, built upon the Magistrate's Authority, might not (against Conscience) be imposed upon the Worshippers of God? For the greatest part of these Ceremonies and Superstitions consists in the Religious Use of such things as are in their own nature indifferent: nor are they sinful upon any other account than because God is not the Author of them. The sprinkling of Water, and the use of Bread and Wine, are both in their own nature, and in the ordinary occasions of Life, altogether indifferent. Will any man therefore say that these things could have been introduced into Religion, and made a part of Divine Worship, if not by Divine Institution? If any Human Authority or Civil Power could have done this, why might it not also injoyn the eating of Fish, the drinking of Ale, in the holy Banquet, as a part of Divine Worship? Why not the sprinkling of the Blood of Beasts in Churches, and Expiations by Water or Fire, and abundance more of this kind? But these things, how indifferent soever they be in common uses, when they come to be annexed unto Divine Worship, without Divine Authority, they are as abominable to God, as the Sacrifice of a Dog. And why a Dog so abominable? What difference is there between a Dog and a Goat, in respect of the Divine Nature, equally and infinitely distant from all Affinity with Matter; unless it be that God required the use of the one in his Worship, and not of the other? We see therefore that indifferent things how much soever they be under the Power of the Civil Magistrate, yet cannot upon that pretence be introduced into Religion, and imposed upon Religious Assemblies; because in the Worship of God they wholly cease to be indifferent. He that worships God does it with design to please him and procure his favour. But that cannot be done by him, who, upon the command of another, offers unto God that which he knows will be displeasing to him, because not commanded by himself. This is not to please God, or appease his Wrath, but willingly and knowingly to provoke him, by a manifest Contempt; which is a thing absolutely repugnant to the nature and end of Worship.

But it will here be asked: If nothing belonging to Divine Worship be left to human Discretion, how is it then that Churches themselves have the power of ordering any thing about the Time and Place of Worship, and the like? To this I answer; That in Religious Worship we must distinguish between what is part of the Worship it self, and what is but a Circumstance. That is a part of the Worship which is believed to be appointed by God; and to be well-pleasing to him; and therefore that is necessary. Circumstances are such things which, tho' in general they cannot be separated from Worship, yet the particular instances or modifications of them are not determined; and therefore they are indifferent. Of this sort are the Time and Place of Worship, the Habit and Posture of him that worships. These are Circumstances, and perfectly indifferent, where God has not given any express Command about them. For example: Amongst the *Jews,* the Time and Place of their Worship, and the Habits of those that officiated in it, were not meer Circumstances, but a part of the Worship it self; in which if any thing were defective, or different from that Institution, they could not hope that it would be accepted by God. But these, to Christians under the liberty of the Gospel, are meer Circumstances of Worship, which the Prudence of every Church may bring into such use as shall be judged most subservient to the end of Order, Decency, and Edification. But, even under the Gospel, those who believe the First, or the Seventh Day to be set apart by God, and consecrated still to his Worship, to them that Portion of Time is not a simple Circumstance, but a Real Part of Divine Worship, which can neither be changed or neglected.

In the next place: As the Magistrate has no Power to *impose* by his Laws, the use of any Rites and Ceremonies in any Church, so neither has he any Power to *forbid* the use of such Rites and Ceremonies as are already received, approved, and practised by any Church: Because if he did so, he would destroy the Church it self; the end of whose Institution is only to worship God with freedom, after its own manner.

You will say, by this Rule, if some Congregations should have a mind to sacrifice Infants, or (as the Primitive Christians were falsely accused) lustfully pollute themselves in promiscuous Uncleanness, or practise any other such heinous Enormities, is the Magistrate obliged to tolerate them, because they are committed in a Religious Assembly? I answer, No. These things are not lawful in the ordinary course of life, nor in any private house; and therefore neither are they so in the Worship of God, or in any religious Meeting. But indeed if any People congregated upon account of Religion, should be desirous to sacrifice a Calf, I deny that That ought to be prohibited by a Law. *Melibaeus,* whose Calf it is, may lawfully kill his Calf at home and burn any part of it that he thinks fit. For no Injury is thereby done to any one, no prejudice to another mans Goods. And for the same reason he may kill his Calf also in a religious Meeting. Whether the doing so be well-pleasing to God or no, it is their part to consider that do it. The part of the Magistrate is only to take care that the Commonwealth receive no prejudice, and that there be no Injury done to any man, either in Life or Estate. And thus what may be spent on a Feast, may be spent on a Sacrifice. But if peradventure such were the state of things, that the Interest of the Commonwealth required all slaughter of Beasts should be forborn for some while, in order to the increasing of the stock of Cattel, that had been destroyed by some extraordinary Murrain; Who sees not that the Magistrate, in such a case, may forbid all his Subjects to kill any Calves for any use whatsoever? Only 'tis to be observed, that in this case the Law is not made about a Religious, but a Political matter: nor is the Sacrifice, but the Slaughter of Calves thereby prohibited.

By this we see what difference there is between the Church and the Commonwealth. Whatsoever is lawful in the Commonwealth, cannot be prohibited by the Magistrate in the Church. Whatsoever is permitted unto any of his Subjects for their ordinary use, neither can nor ought to be forbidden by him to any Sect of People for their religious Uses. If any man may lawfully take Bread or Wine, either sitting or kneeling, in his own house, the Law ought not to abridge him of the same Liberty in his Religious Worship; tho' in the Church the use of Bread and Wine be very different, and be there applied to the Mysteries of Faith, and Rites of Divine Worship. But those things that are prejudicial to the Commonweal of a People in their ordinary use, and are therefore forbidden by Laws, those things ought not to be permitted to Churches in their sacred Rites. Onely the Magistrate ought always to be very careful that he do not misuse his Authority, to the oppression of any Church, under pretence of publick Good.

It may be said; What if a Church be *Idolatrous,* is that also to be tolerated by the Magistrate? I answer. What Power can be given to the Magistrate for the suppression of an Idolatrous Church, which may not, in time and place, be made use of to the ruine of an Orthodox one? For it must be remembered that the Civil Power is the same every where and the Religion of every Prince is Orthodox to himself. If therefore such a Power be granted unto the Civil Magistrate in Spirituals, as that at *Geneva* (for Example) he may extirpate, by Violence and Blood,

the Religion which is there reputed Idolatrous; by the same Rule another Magistrate, in some neighbouring Country, may oppress the Re-
formed Religion; and, in *India,* the Christian. The Civil Power can
either change every thing in Religion, according to the Prince's pleasure, or it can change nothing. If it be once permitted to introduce any
thing into Religion, by the means of Laws and Penalties, there can be
no bounds put to it; but it will in the same manner be lawful to alter
every thing, according to that Rule of Truth which the Magistrate has
framed unto himself. No man whatsoever ought therefore to be deprived of his Terrestrial Enjoyments, upon account of his Religion. Not
even *Americans,* subjected unto a Christian Prince, are to be punished
either in Body or Goods, for not imbracing our Faith and Worship. If
they are perswaded that they please God in observing the Rites of their
own Country, and that they shall obtain Happiness by that means, they
are to be left unto God and themselves. Let us trace this matter to the
bottom. Thus it is. An inconsiderable and weak number of Christians,
destitute of every thing, arrive in a Pagan Country: These Foreigners
beseech the Inhabitants, by the bowels of Humanity, that they would
succour them with the necessaries of life: Those necessaries are given
them; Habitations are granted; and they all joyn together, and grow up
into one Body of People. The Christian Religion by this means takes
root in that Countrey, and spreads it self; but does not suddenly grow
the strongest. While things are in this condition, Peace, Friendship,
Faith and equal Justice, are preserved amongst them. At length the
Magistrate becomes a Christian, and by that means their Party becomes the most powerful. Then immediately all Compacts are to be
broken, all Civil Rights to be violated, that Idolatry may be extirpated:
And unless these innocent Pagans, strict Observers of the Rules of
Equity and the Law of Nature, and no ways offending against the Laws
of the Society, I say unless they will forsake their ancient Religion, and
embrace a new and strange one, they are to be turned out of the Lands
and Possessions of their Forefathers, and perhaps deprived of Life it
self. Then at last it appears what Zeal for the Church, joyned with the
desire of Dominion, is capable to produce; and how easily the pretence
of Religion, and of the care of Souls, serves for a Cloak to Covetousness, Rapine, and Ambition.

Now whosoever maintains that Idolatry is to be rooted out of any
place by Laws, Punishments, Fire, and Sword, may apply this Story to
himself. For the reason of the thing is equal, both in *America* and
Europe. And neither Pagans there, nor any Dissenting Christians here,
can with any right be deprived of their worldly Goods, by the pre-
dominating Faction of a Court-Church: nor are any Civil Rights to be
either changed or violated upon account of Religion in one place more
than another.

But *Idolatry* (say some) is a sin, and therefore not to be tolerated. If
they said it were therefore to be avoided, the Inference were good. But
it does not follow, that because it is a sin it ought therefore to be punished by the Magistrate. For it does not belong unto the Magistrate to

make use of his Sword in punishing every thing, indifferently, that he takes to be a sin against God. Covetousness, Uncharitableness, Idleness, and many other things are sins, by the consent of all men, which yet no man ever said were to be punished by the Magistrate. The reason is, because they are not prejudicial to other mens Rights, nor do they break the publick Peace of Societies. Nay, even the sins of Lying and Perjury, are no where punishable by Laws; unless in certain cases, in which the real Turpitude of the thing, and the offence against God, are not considered, but only the Injury done unto mens Neighbours, and to the Commonwealth. And what if in another Country, to a Mahumetan or a Pagan Prince, the Christian Religion seem false and offensive to God; may not the Christians for the same reason, and after the same manner, be extirpated there?

But it may be urged further, That by the Law of *Moses* Idolaters were to be rooted out. True indeed, by the Law of *Moses*. But that is not obligatory to us Christians. No body pretends that every thing, generally, enjoyned by the Law of *Moses,* ought to be practised by Christians. But there is nothing more frivolous than that common distinction of Moral, Judicial, and Ceremonial Law, which men ordinarily make use of. For no positive Law whatsoever can oblige any People but those to whom it is given. *Hear O Israel;* sufficiently restrains the Obligation of the Law of *Moses* only to that People. And this Consideration alone is Answer enough unto those that urge the Authority of the Law of *Moses;* for the inflicting of Capital Punishments upon Idolaters. But however, I will examine this Argument a little more particularly.

The Case of Idolaters, in respect of the *Jewish* Commonwealth, falls under a double consideration. The first is of those Who, being initiated in the *Mosaical* Rites, and made Citizens of that Commonwealth, did afterwards apostatise from the Worship of the God of *Israel*. These were proceeded against as Traytors and Rebels, guilt of no less than High-treason. For the Commonwealth of the *Jews,* different in that from all others, was an absolute Theocracy: nor was there, or could there be, any difference between that Commonwealth and the Church. The Laws established there concerning the Worship of One Invisible Deity, were the Civil Laws of that People, and a part of their Political Government; in which God himself was the Legislator. Now if any one can shew me where there is a Commonwealth, at this time, constituted upon that Foundation, I will acknowledge that the Ecclesiastical Laws do there unavoidably become a part of the Civil; and that the Subjects of that Government both may, and ought to be kept in strict conformity with that Church, by the Civil Power. But there is absolutely no such thing, under the Gospel, as a Christian Commonwealth. There are, indeed, many Cities and Kingdoms that have embraced the Faith of Christ; but they have retained their ancient Form of Government; with which the Law of Christ hath not at all medled. He, indeed, hath taught men how, by Faith and Good Works, they may attain Eternal Life. But he instituted no Commonwealth. He prescribed unto his Followers no new and peculiar Form of Government; Nor put he the Sword into any Magistrate's Hand, with Commission to make use of it in forcing men to forsake their former Religion, and receive his.

Secondly. Foreigners, and such as were Strangers to the Commonwealth of *Israel,* were not compell'd by force to observe the Rites of the *Mosaical* Law. But, on the contrary, in the very same place where it is ordered that *an Israelite that was an Idolater should be put to death,* there it is provided that *Strangers should not be vexed nor oppressed.*[7] I confess that the Seven Nations that possest the Land which was promised to the *Israelites,* were utterly to be cut off. But this was not singly because they were Idolators. For, if that had been the Reason, why were the *Moabites* and other Nations to be spared? No; the Reason is this. God being in a peculiar manner the King of the *Jews,* he could not suffer the Adoration of any other Deity (which was properly an Act of High-treason against himself) in the Land of *Canaan,* which was his Kingdom. For such a manifest Revolt could no ways consist with his Dominion, which was perfectly Political, in that Country. All Idolatry was therefore to be rooted out of the Bounds of his Kingdom; because it was an acknowledgment of another God, that is to say, another King; against the Laws of Empire. The Inhabitants were also to be driven out, that the intire possession of the Land might be given to the *Israelites.* And for the like Reason the *Emims* and the *Horims* were driven out of their Countries, by the Children of *Esau* and *Lot;*[8] and their Lands, upon the same grounds, given by God to the Invaders. But tho all Idolatry was thus rooted out of the Land of *Canaan,* yet every Idolater was not brought to Execution. The whole Family of *Rahab,* the whole Nation of the *Gibeonites,* articled with *Josuah,* and were allowed by Treaty: and there were many Captives amongst the *Jews,* who were Idolaters. *David and Solomon* subdued many Countries without the Confines of the Land of Promise, and carried their Conquests as far as *Euphrates.* Amongst so many Captives taken, so many Nations reduced under their Obedience, we find not one man forced into the Jewish Religion, and the Worship of the True God, and punished for Idolatry, tho all of them were certainly guilty of it. If any one indeed, becoming a Proselyte, desired to be made a Denison of their Commonwealth, he was obliged to submit unto their Laws; that is, to embrace their Religion. But this he did willingly, on his own accord, not by constraint. He did not unwillingly submit, to shew his Obedience; But he sought and sollicited for it, as a Privilege. And as soon as he was admitted, he became subject to the Laws of the Commonwealth, by which all Idolatry was forbidden within the Borders of the Land of *Canaan.* But that Law (as I have said) did not reach to any of those Regions, however subjected unto the *Jews,* that were situated without those Bounds.

7. Exod. 22.20,21.

8. Deut. 2.

Thus far concerning outward Worship. Let us now consider *Articles of Faith.*

The *Articles* of Religion are some of them *Practical,* and some *Speculative.* Now, tho both sorts consist in the Knowledge of Truth, yet these terminate simply in the Understanding, Those influence the Will and Manners. Speculative Opinions, therefore, and *Articles of Faith* (as they are called) which are required only to be believed, cannot be imposed on any Church by the Law of the Land. For it is absurd that things should be enjoyned by Laws, which are not in mens power to perform. And to believe this or that to be true, does not depend upon our Will. But of this enough has been said already. But (will some say) let men at least profess that they believe. A sweet Religion indeed, that obliges men to dissemble, and tell Lies both to God and Man, for the Salvation of their Souls! If the Magistrate thinks to save men thus, he seems to understand little of the way of Salvation. And if he does it not in order to save them, why is he so sollicitous about the Articles of Faith as to enact them by a Law?

Further, The Magistrate ought not to forbid the Preaching or Professing of any Speculative Opinions in any Church, because they have no manner of relation to the Civil Rights of the Subjects. If a *Roman Catholick* believe that to be really the Body of Christ, which another man calls Bread, he does no injury thereby to his Neighbour. If a *Jew* do not believe the New Testament to be the Word of God, he does not thereby alter any thing in mens Civil Rights. If a Heathen doubt of both Testaments, he is not therefore to be punished as a pernicious Citizen. The Power of the Magistrate, and the Estates of the People, may be equally secure, whether any man believe these things or no. I readily grant, that these Opinions are false and absurd. But the business of Laws is not to provide for the Truth of Opinions, but for the Safety and Security of the Commonwealth, and of every particular mans Goods and Person. And so it ought to be. For Truth certainly would do well enough, if she were once left to shift for her self. She seldom has received, and I fear never will receive much Assistance from the Power of Great men, to whom she is but rarely known, and more rarely welcome. She is not taught by Laws, nor has she any need of Force to procure her entrance into the minds of men. Errors indeed prevail by the assistance of forreign and borrowed Succours. But if Truth makes not her way into the Understanding by her own Light she will be but the weaker for any borrowed force Violence can add to her. Thus much for Speculative Opinions. Let us now proceed to *Practical* ones.

A Good Life, in which consists not the least part of Religion and true Piety, concerns also the Civil Government: and in it lies the safety both of Mens Souls, and of the Commonwealth. Moral Actions belong therefore to the Jursidiction both of the outward and inward Court; both of the Civil and Domestick Governor; I mean, both of the Magistrate and Conscience. Here therefore is great danger, least one of these Jursidictions intrench upon the other, and Discord arise between the Keeper of the publick Peace and the Overseers of Souls. But if what has been already said concerning the Limits of both these Governments be rightly considered, it will easily remove all difficulty in this matter.

Every man has an Immortal Soul, capable of Eternal Happiness or Misery; whose Happiness depending upon his believing and doing those things in this Life, which are necessary to the obtaining of Gods Favour, and are prescribed by God to that end; it follows from thence, *1st,* That the observance of these things is the highest Obligation that lies upon Mankind, and that our utmost Care, Application, and Diligence, ought to be exercised in the Search and Performance of them; Because there is nothing in this World that is of any consideration in comparison with Eternity. *2dly,* That seeing one Man does not violate the Right of another, by his Erroneous Opinions, and undue manner of Worship, nor is his Perdition any prejudice to another Mans Affairs; therefore the care of each Mans Salvation belongs only to himself. But I would not have this understood, as if I meant hereby to condemn all charitable Admonitions, and affectionate Endeavours to reduce Men from Errors; which are indeed the greatest Duty of a Christian. Any one many employ as many Exhortations and Arguments as he pleases, towards the promoting of another man's Salvation. But all Force and Compulsion are to be forborn. Nothing is to be done imperiously. No body is obliged in that matter to yield Obedience unto the Admonitions or Injunctions of another, further than he himself is perswaded. Every man, in that, has the supreme and absolute Authority of judging for himself. And the Reason is, because no body else is concerned in it, nor can receive any prejudice from his Conduct therein.

But besides their Souls, which are Immortal, Men have also their Temporal Lives here upon Earth; the State whereof being frail and fleeting, and the duration uncertain; they have need of several outward Conveniences to the support thereof, which are to be procured or preserved by Pains and industry. For those things that are necessary to the comfortable support of our Lives are not the spontaneous Products of Nature, nor do offer themselves fit and prepared for our use. This part therefore draws on another care, and necessarily gives another Imployment. But the pravity of Mankind being such, that they had rather injuriously prey upon the Fruits of other Mens Labours, than take pains to provide for themselves; the necessity of preserving Men in the Possession of what honest industry has already acquired, and also of preserving their Liberty and strength, whereby they may acquire what they further want; obliges Men to enter into Society with one another; that by mutual Assistance, and joint Force, they may secure unto each other their Proprieties in the things that contribute to the Comfort and Happiness of this Life; leaving in the mean while to every Man the care of his own Eternal Happiness, the attainment whereof can neither be facilitated by another Mans Industry, nor can the loss of it turn to another Mans Prejudice, nor the hope of it be forced from him by any external Violence. But forasmuch as Men thus entring into Societies, grounded upon their mutual Compacts of Assistance, for the Defence of their Temporal Goods, may nevertheless be deprived of them, either by the Rapine and Fraud of their Fellow-Citizens, or by the hostile Violence of Forreigners; the Remedy of this Evil consists in Arms, Riches, and Multitude of Citizens; the Remedy of the other in Laws; and the Care of all things relating both to the one and the other, is committed by the Society to the Civil Magistrate. This is the Original, this is the Use, and these are the Bounds of the Legislative (which is the Supreme) Power, in every Commonwealth. I mean, that Provision may be made for the security of each Mans private Possessions; for the Peace, Riches, and publick Commodities of the whole People; and, as much as possible, for the Increase of their inward Strength, against Forreign Invasions.

These things being thus explain'd, it is easie to understand to what end the Legislative Power ought to be directed, and by what Measures regulated; and that is the Temporal Good and outward Prosperity of the Society; which is the sole Reason of Mens entring into Society, and the only thing they seek and aim at in it. And it is also evident what Liberty remains to Men in reference to their eternal Salvation, and that is, that every one should do what he in his Conscience is perswaded to be acceptable to the Almighty, on whose good pleasure and acceptance depends their eternal Happiness. For Obedience is due in the first place to God, and afterwards to the Laws.

But some may ask, *What if the Magistrate should enjoyn any thing by his Authority that appears unlawful to the Conscience of a private Person?* I answer, That if Government be faithfully administred, and the Counsels of the Magistrate be indeed directed to the publick Good, this will seldom happen. But if perhaps it do so fall out; I say, that such a private Person is to abstain from the Action that he judges unlawful; and he is to undergo the Punishment, which it is not unlawful for him to bear. For the private judgment of any Person concerning a Law enacted in Political Matters, for the publick Good, does not take away the Obligation of that Law, nor deserve a Dispensation. But if the Law indeed be concerning things that lie not within the Verge of the Magistrate's Authority; (as for Example, that the People, or any Party amongst them, should be compell'd to embrace a strange Religion, and join in the Worship and Ceremonies of another Church,) men are not in these cases obliged by that Law, against their Consciences. For the Political Society is instituted for no other end but only to secure every mans Possession of the things of this life. The care of each mans Soul and of the things of Heaven, which neither does belong to the Commonwealth, nor can be subjected to it, is left entirely to every mans self. Thus the safeguard of mens lives, and of the things that belong unto this life, is the business of the Commonwealth; and the preserving of those things unto their Owners is the Duty of the Magistrate. And therefore the Magistrate cannot take away these worldly things from this man, or party, and give them to that; nor change Propriet amongst Fellow-Subjects, (no not even by a Law) for a cause that has no relation to the end of Civil Government; I mean, for their Religion which whether it be true or false, does no prejudice to the worldl concerns of their Fellow-Subjects, which are the things that only belong unto the care of the Commonwealth.

But what if the Magistrate believe such a Law as this to be for the publick Good? I answer: As the private Judgment of any particular Person, if erroneous, does not exempt him from the obligation of Law, so the private Judgment (as I may call it) of the Magistrate does not give him any new Right of imposing Laws upon his subjects, which neither was in the Constitution of the Government granted him, nor ever was in the power of the People to grant: much less, if he make it his business to enrich and advance his Followers and Fellow-sectaries, with the Spoils of others. But what if the Magistrate believe that he has the Right to make such Laws, and that they are for the publick Good; and his Subjects believe the contrary? Who shall be Judge between them? I answer, God alone. For there is no Judge upon earth between the Supreme Magistrate and the People. God, I say, is the only Judge in this case, who will retribute unto every one at the last day according to his Deserts; that is, according to his sincerity and uprightness in endeavouring to promote Piety, and the publick Weal and Peace of Mankind. But what shall be done in the mean while? I answer: The principal and chief care of every one ought to be of his own Soul first, and in the next place of the publick Peace: tho' yet there are very few will think 'tis Peace there, where they see all laid waste.

There are two sorts of Contests amongst men; the one managed by Law, the other by Force: and these are of that nature, that where the one ends, the other always begins. But it is not my business to inquire into the Power of the Magistrate in the different Constitutions of Nations. I only know what usually happens where Controversies arise, without a Judge to determine them. You will say then the Magistrate being the stronger will have his Will, and carry his point. Without doubt. But the Question is not here concerning the doubtfulness of the Event, but the Rule of Right.

But to come to particulars. I say, *First,* No Opinions contrary to human Society, or to those moral Rules which are necessary to the preservation of Civil Society, are to be tolerated by the Magistrate. But of these indeed Examples in any Church are rare. For no Sect can easily arrive to such a degree of madness, as that it should think fit to teach, for Doctrines of Religion, such things as manifestly undermine the Foundations of Society, and are therefore condemned by the Judgment of all Mankind: because their own Interest, Peace, Reputation, every Thing, would be thereby endangered.

Another more secret Evil, but more dangerous to the Commonwealth, is, when men arrogate to themselves, and to those of their own Sect, some peculiar Prerogative, covered over with a specious shew of deceitful words, but in effect opposite to the Civil Right of the Community. For Example. We cannot find any Sect that teaches expressly, and openly, that men are not obliged to keep their Promise; that Princes may be dethroned by those that differ from them in Religion; or that the Dominion of all things belongs only to themselves. For these things, proposed thus nakedly and plainly, would soon draw on them the Eye and Hand of the Magistrate, and awaken all the care of the Commonwealth to a watchfulness against the spreading of so dangerous an Evil. But nevertheless, we find those that say the same things, in other words. What else do they mean, who teach that *Faith is not to be kept with Hereticks?* Their meaning, forsooth, is that the privilege of breaking Faith belongs unto themselves: For they declare all that are not of their Communion to be Hereticks, or at least may declare them so whensoever they think fit. What can be the meaning of their asserting that *Kings excommunicated forfeit their Crowns and Kingdoms?* It is evident that they thereby arrogate unto themselves the Power of deposing Kings: because they challenge the Power of Excommunication, as the peculiar Right of their Hierarchy. That *Dominion is founded in Grace,* is also an Assertion by which those that maintain it do plainly lay claim to the possession of all things. For they are not so wanting to themselves as not to believe, or at least as not to profess, themselves to be the truly pious and faithful. These therefore, and the like, who attribute unto the Faithful, Religious and Orthodox, that is, in plain terms, unto themselves, any peculiar Privilege of Power above other Mortals, in Civil Concernments; or who, upon pretence of Religion, do challenge any manner of Authority over such, as are not associated with them in the Ecclesiastical Communion; I say these have no right to be tolerated by the Magistrate; as neither those that will not own and teach the Duty of tolerating All men in matters of meer Religion. For what do all these and the like Doctrines signifie, but that they may, and are ready upon any occasion to seise the Government, and possess themselves of the Estates and Fortunes of their Fellow-Subjects; and that they only ask leave to be tolerated by the Magistrate so long until they find themselves strong enough to effect it?

Again: That Church can have no right to be tolerated by the Magistrate, which is constituted upon such a bottom, that all those who enter into it, do thereby, *ipso facto,* deliver themselves up to the Protection and Service of another Prince. For by this means the Magistrate would give way to the settling of a forreign Jurisdiction in his own Country, and suffer his own People to be listed, as it were, for Souldiers against his own Government. Nor does the frivolous and fallacious distinction between the Court and the Church afford any remedy to this Inconvenience; especially when both the one and the other are equally subject to the absolute Authority of the same person; who has not only power to perswade the Members of his Church to whatsoever he lists either as purely Religious, or in order thereunto, but can also enjoyn it them on pain of Eternal Fire. It is ridiculous for any one to profess himself to be a *Mahumetan* only in his Religion, but in every thing else a faithful Subject to a Christian Magistrate, whilst at the same time he acknowledges himself bound to yield blind obedience to the *Mufti* of *Constantinople;* who himself is intirely obedient to the *Ottoman* Emperor, and frames the feigned Oracles of that Religion according to his pleasure. But this Mahumetan living among Christians, would yet more apparently renounce their Government, if he acknowledged the same Person to be Head of his Church who is the Supreme Magistrate in the State.

Lastly, Those are not at all to be tolerated who deny the Being of a God. Promises, Covenants, and Oaths, which are the Bonds of Humane Society, can have no hold upon an Atheist. The taking away of God, tho but even in thought, dissolves all. Besides also, those that by their Atheism undermine and destroy all Religion, can have no pretence of Religion whereupon to challenge the Privilege of a Toleration. As for other Practical Opinions, tho not absolutely free from all Error, if they do not tend to establish Domination over others, or Civil Impunity to the Church in which they are taught, there can be no Reason why they should not be tolerated.

It remains that I say something concerning those Assemblies, which being vulgarly called, and perhaps having sometimes been *Conventicles,* and Nurseries of Factions and Seditions, are thought to afford the strongest matter of Objection against this Doctrine of Toleration. But this has not happened by anything peculiar unto the Genius of such Assemblies, but by the unhappy Circumstances of an oppressed or ill-setled Liberty. These Accusations would soon cease, if the Law of Toleration were once so setled, that all Churches were obliged to lay down Toleration as the Foundation of their own Liberty; and teach that Liberty of Conscience is every mans natural Right, equally belonging to Dissenters as to themselves; and that no body ought to be compelled in matters of Religion, either by Law or Force. The Establishment of this one thing would take away all ground of Complaints and Tumults upon account of Conscience. And these Causes of Discontents and Animosities being once removed, there would remain nothing in these Assemblies that were not more peaceable, and less apt to produce Disturbance of State, than in any other Meetings whatsoever. But let us examine particularly the Heads of these Accusations.

You'll say, That *Assemblies and Meetings endanger the Publick Peace, and threaten the Commonwealth.* I answer: If this be so, Why are there daily such numerous Meetings in Markets, and Courts of Judicature? Why are Crowds upon the Exchange, and a Concourse of People in Cities suffered? You'll reply; Those are Civil Assemblies; but These we object against, are Ecclesiastical. I answer: 'Tis a likely thing indeed, that such Assemblies as are altogether remote from Civil Affairs, should be most apt to embroyl them. O, but Civil Assemblies are composed of men that differ from one another in matters of Religion; but these Ecclesiastical Meetings are of Persons that are all of one Opinion. As if an Agreement in matters of Religion, were in effect a Conspiracy against the Commonwealth; or as if men would not be so much the more warmly unanimous in Religion, the less liberty they had of Assembling. But it will be urged still, That Civil Assemblies are open, and free for any one to enter into; whereas Religious Conventicles are more private, and thereby give opportunity to Clandestine Machinations. I answer, That this is not strictly true: For many Civil

Assemblies are not open to every one. And if some Religious Meetings be private, Who are they (I beseech you) that are to be blamed for it? those that desire, or those that forbid their being publick? Again; You'll say, That Religious Communion does exceedingly unite mens Minds and Affections to one another, and is therefore the more dangerous. But if this be so, Why is not the Magistrate afraid of his own Church; and why does he not forbid their Assemblies, as things dangerous to his Government? You'll say, Because he himself is a Part, and even the Head of them. As if he were not also a Part of the Commonwealth, and the Head of the whole People.

Let us therefore deal plainly. The Magistrate is afraid of other Churches, but not of his own; because he is kind and favourable to the one, but severe and cruel to the other. These he treats like Children, and indulges them even to Wantonness. Those he uses as Slaves; and how blamelessly soever they demean themselves, recompenses them no otherwise than by Gallies, Prisons, Confiscations, and Death. These he cherishes and defends: Those he continually scourges and oppresses. Let him turn the Tables: Or let those Dissenters enjoy but the same Privileges in Civils as his other Subjects, and he will quickly find that these Religious Meetings will be no longer dangerous. For if men enter into Seditious Conspiracies, 'tis not Religion that inspires them to it in their Meetings; but their Sufferings and Oppressions that make them willing to ease themselves. Just and moderate Governments are every where quiet, every where safe. But Oppression raises Ferments, and makes men struggle to cast off an uneasie and tyrannical Yoke. I know that Seditions are very frequently raised, upon pretence of Religion. But 'tis as true that, for Religion, Subjects are frequently ill treated, and live miserably. Believe me, the Stirs that are made, proceed not from any peculiar Temper of this or that Church or Religious Society; but from the common Disposition of all Mankind, who when they groan under any heavy Burthen, endeavour naturally to shake off the Yoke that galls their Necks. Suppose this Business of Religion were let alone, and that there were some other Distinction made between men and men, upon account of their different Complexions, Shapes, and Features, so that those who have black Hair (for example) or gray Eyes, should not enjoy the same Privileges as other Citizens; that they should not be permitted either to buy or sell, or live by their Callings; that Parents should not have the Government and Education of their own Children; that all should either be excluded from the Benefit of the Laws, or meet with partial Judges; can it be doubted but these Persons thus distinguished from others by the Colour of their Hair and Eyes and united together by one common Persecution, would be as dangerous to the Magistrate, as any others that had associated themselves meerly upon the account of Religion? Some enter into Company for Trade and Profit: Others, for want of Business, have their Clubs for Clarret. Neighbourhood joyns some, and Religion others. But there is one only thing which gathers People into Seditious Commotions, and that is Oppression.

You'll say; What, will you have People to meet at Divine Service *against the Magistrates Will?* I answer; Why, I pray, against his Will? Is it not both lawful and necessary that they should meet? Against his Will, do you say? That's what I complain of. That is the very Root of all the Mischief. Why are Assemblies less sufferable in a Church than in a Theater or Market? Those that meet there are not either more vicious, or more turbulent, than those that meet elsewhere. The Business in that is, that they are ill used, and therefore they are not to be suffered. Take away the Partiality that is used towards them in matters of Common Right; change the Laws, take away the Penalties unto which they are subjected, and all things will immediately become safe and peaceable; Nay, those that are averse to the Religion of the Magistrate, will think themselves so much the more bound to maintain the Peace of the Commonwealth, as their Condition is better in that place than elsewhere; And all the several separate Congregations, like so many Guardians of the Publick Peace, will watch one another, that nothing may be innovated or changed in the Form of the Government: Because they can hope for nothing better than what they already enjoy; that is, an equal Condition with their Fellow-Subjects, under a just and moderate Government. Now if that Church, which agrees in Religion with the Prince, be esteemed the chief Support of any Civil Government, and that for no other Reason (as has already been shewn) than because the Prince is kind, and the Laws are favourable to it; how much greater will be the Security of a Government, where all good Subjects, of whatsoever Church they be, without any Distinction upon account of Religion, enjoying the same Favour of the Prince, and the same Benefit of the Laws, shall become the common Support and Guard of it; and where none will have any occasion to fear the Severity of the Laws, but those that do Injuries to their Neighbours, and offend against the Civil Peace?

That we may draw towards a Conclusion. The *Sum of all* we drive at is, *That every Man may enjoy the same Rights that are granted to others.* Is it permitted to worship God in the *Roman* manner? Let it be permitted to do it in the *Geneva* Form also. Is it permitted to speak *Latin* in the Market-place? Let those that have a mind to it, be permitted to do it also in the Church. Is it lawfull for any man in his own House, to kneel, stand, sit, or use any other Posture; and to cloath himself in White or Black, in short or in long Garments? Let it not be made unlawful to eat Bread, drink Wine, or wash with Water, in the Church. In a Word: Whatsoever things are left free by Law in the common occasions of Life, let them remain free unto every Church in Divine Worship. Let no Mans Life, or Body, or House, or Estate, suffer any manner of Prejudice upon these Accounts. Can you allow of the *Presbyterian* Discipline? Why should not the *Episcopal* also have what they like? Ecclesiastical Authority, whether it be administered by the Hands of a Single Person, or many, is every where the same; and neither has any Jurisdiction in things Civil, nor any manner of Power of Compulsion, nor any thing at all to do with Riches and Revenues.

Ecclesiastical Assemblies, and Sermons, are justified by daily experience, and publick allowance. These are allowed to People of some one Perswasion: Why not to all? If any thing pass in a Religious Meeting seditiously, and contrary to the publick Peace, it is to be punished in the same manner, and no otherwise, than as if it had happened in a Fair or Market. These Meetings ought not to be Sanctuaries for Factious and Flagitious Fellows: Nor ought it to be less lawful for Men to meet in Churches than in Halls: Nor are one part of the Subjects to be esteemed more blameable, for their meeting together, than others. Every one is to be accountable for his own Actions; and no Man is to be laid under a Suspicion, or Odium, for the Fault of another. Those that are Seditious, Murderers, Thieves, Robbers, Adulterers, Slanderers, etc. of whatsoever Church, whether National or not, ought to be punished and suppressed. But those whose Doctrine is peaceable, and whose Manners are pure and blameless, ought to be upon equal Terms with their Fellow-Subjects. Thus if Solemn Assemblies, Observations of Festivals, publick Worship, be permitted to any one sort of Professors; all these things ought to be permitted to the *Presbyterians, Independents, Anabaptists, Arminians, Quakers*, and others, with the same Liberty. Nay, if we may openly speak the Truth, and as becomes one Man to another, neither *Pagan*, nor *Mahumetan*, nor *Jew*, ought to be excluded from the Civil Rights of the Commonwealth, because of his Religion. The Gospel commands no such thing. The Church, which *judges not those that are without*, wants it not.[9] And the Commonwealth, which embraces indifferently all Men that are honest, peaceable and industrious, requires it not. Shall we suffer a *Pagan* to deal and trade with us, and shall we not suffer him to pray unto and worship God? If we allow the *Jews* to have private Houses and Dwellings amongst us, Why should we not allow them to have Synagogues? Is their Doctrine more false, their Worship more abominable, or is the Civil Peace more endangered, by their meeting in publick than in their private Houses? But if these things may be granted to *Jews* and *Pagans*, surely the condition of any Christians ought not to be worse than theirs in a Christian Commonwealth.

You'll say, perhaps, Yes, it ought to be: Because they are inclinable to Factions, Tumults, and Civil Wars. I answer: Is this the fault of the Christian Religion? If it be so, truly the Christian Religion is the worst of all Religions, and ought neither to be embraced by any particular Person, nor tolerated by any Commonwealth. For if this be the Genius, this the Nature of the Christian Religion, to be turbulent, and destructive to the Civil Peace, that Church it self which the Magistrate indulges will not always be innocent. But far be it from us to say any such thing of that Religion, which carries the greatest opposition to Covetousness, Ambition, Discord, Contention, and all manner of inordinate Desires; and is the most modest and peaceable Religion that ever was. We must therefore seek another Cause of those Evils that are

9. 1 Cor. 5.12, 13

charged upon Religion. And if we consider right, we shall find it to consist wholly in the Subject that I am treating of. It is not the diversity of Opinions, (which cannot be avoided) but the refusal of Toleration to those that are of different Opinions, (which might have been granted) that has produced all the Bustles and Wars, that have been in the Christian World, upon account of Religion. The Heads and Leaders of the Church, moved by Avarice and insatiable desire of Dominion, making use of the immoderate Ambition of Magistrates, and the credulous Supersition of the giddy Multitude, have incensed and animated them against those that dissent from themselves; by preaching unto them, contrary to the Laws of the Gospel and to the Precepts of Charity, That Schismaticks and Hereticks are to be outed of their Possessions, and destroyed. And thus have they mixed together and confounded two things that are in themselves most different, the Church and the Commonwealth. Now as it is very difficult for men patiently to suffer themselves to be stript of the Goods, which they have got by their honest Industry; and contrary to all the Laws of Equity, both Humane and Divine, to be delivered up for a Prey to other mens Violence and Rapine; especially when they are otherwise altogether blameless; and that the Occasion for which they are thus treated does not at all belong to the Jurisdiction of the Magistrate; but intirely to the Conscience of every particular man; for the Conduct of which he is accountable to God only; What else can be expected, but that these men, growing weary of the Evils under which they labour, should in the end think it lawful for them to resist Force with Force, and to defend their natural Rights (which are not forfeitable upon account of Religion) with Arms as well as they can? That this has been hitherto the ordinary Course of things, is abundantly evident in History: And that it will continue to be so hereafter, is but too apparent in Reason. It cannot indeed be otherwise, so long as the Principle of Persecution for Religion shall prevail, as it has done hitherto, with Magistrate and People; and so long as those that ought to be the Preachers of Peace and Concord, shall continue, with all their Art and Strength, to excite men to Arms, and sound the Trumpet of War. But that Magistrates should thus suffer these Incendiaries, and Disturbers of the Publick Peace, might justly be wondred at; if it did not appear that they have been invited by them unto a Participation of the Spoil, and have therefore thought fit to make use of their Covetousness and Pride as means whereby to increase their own Power. For who does not see that *these Good Men* are indeed more Ministers of the Government, than Ministers of the Gospel; and that by flattering the Ambition, and favouring the Dominion of Princes and men in Authority, they endeavour with all their might to promote that Tyranny in the Commonwealth, which otherwise they should not be able to establish in the Church? This is the unhappy Agreement that we see between the Church and State. Whereas if each of them would contain it self within its own Bounds, the one attending to the worldly Welfare of the Commonwealth, the other to the Salvation of Souls, it is impossible that any Discord should ever have hapned between them.

Sed, pudet haec approbria, etc. God Almighty grant, I beseech him, that the Gospel of Peace may at length be preached, and that Civil Magistrates growing more careful to conform their own Consciences to the Law of God, and less sollicitous about the binding of other mens Consciences by Humane Laws, may, like Fathers of their Country, direct all their Counsels and Endeavours to promote universally the Civil Welfare of all their Children; except only of such as are arrogant, ungovernable, and injurious to their Brethren; and that all Ecclesiastical men, who boast themselves to be the Successors of the Apostles, walking peaceably and modestly in the Apostles steps, without intermedling with State-Affairs, may apply themselves wholly to promote the Salvation of Souls.

Farewell.

Perhaps it may not be amiss to add a few things concerning *Heresy* and *Schism*. A *Turk* is not, nor can be, either Heretick or Schismatick, to a *Christian:* and if any man fall off from the Christian Faith to Mahumetism, he does not thereby become a Heretick or Schismatick, but an Apostate and an Infidel. This no body doubts of. And by this it appears that men of different Religions cannot be Hereticks or Schismaticks to one another.

We are to enquire therefore, what men are of the same Religion. Concerning which, it is manifest that those who have one and the same Rule of Faith and Worship, are of the same Religion: and those who have not the same Rule of Faith and Worship are of different Religions. For since all things that belong unto that Religion are contained in that Rule, it follows necessarily that those who agree in one Rule are of one and the same Religion: and *vice versâ*. Thus Turks and Christians are of different Religions: because these take the *Holy Scriptures* to be the Rule of their Religion, and those the *Alcoran*. And for the same reason, there may be different Religions also even amongst Christians. The *Papists* and the *Lutherans,* tho' both of them profess Faith in Christ, and are therefore called Christians, yet are not both of the same Religion: because These acknowledge nothing but the Holy Scriptures to be the Rule and Foundation of their Religion; Those take in also Traditions and the Decrees of Popes, and of these together make the Rule of their Religion. And thus the Christians of St. *John* (as they are called) and the Christians of *Geneva* are of different Religions: because These also take only the Scriptures; and Those I know not what Traditions, for the Rule of their Religion.

This being setled, it follows; *First,* that Heresy is a Separation made in Ecclesiastical Communion between men of the same Religion, for some Opinions no way contained in the Rule it self. And *Secondly,* that amongst those who acknowledge nothing but the Holy Scriptures to be their Rule of Faith, Heresy is a Separation made in their Christian Communion, for Opinions not contained in the express words of Scripture. Now this Separation may be made in a twofold manner.

1. When the greater part, or (by the Magistrate's Patronage) the stronger part, of the Church separates it self from others, by excluding them out of her Communion, because they will not profess their Belief of certain Opinions which are not the express words of the Scripture. For it is not the paucity of those that are separated, nor the Authority of the Magistrate, that can make any man guilty of Heresy. But he only is an Heretick who divides the Church into parts, introduces Names and Marks of Distinction, and voluntarily makes a Separation because of such Opinions.

2. When any one separates himself from the Communion of a Church, because that Church does not publickly profess some certain Opinions which the Holy Scriptures do not expressly teach.

Both these are *Hereticks: because they err in Fundamentals, and they err obstinately against Knowledge.* For when they have determined the Holy Scriptures to be the only Foundation of Faith, they nevertheless lay down certain Propositions as fundamental, which are not in the Scripture; and because others will not acknowledge these additional Opinions of theirs, nor build upon them as if they were necessary and fundamental, they therefore make a Separation in the Church; either by withdrawing themselves from the others, or expelling the others from them. Nor does it signifie any thing for them to say that their Confessions and Symboles are agreeable to Scripture, and to the Analogy of Faith. For if they be conceived in the express words of Scripture, there can be no question about them; because those things are acknowledged by all Christians to be of Divine Inspiration, and therefore fundamental. But if they say that the Articles which they require to be profess'd, are Consequences deduced from the Scripture; it is undoubtedly well done of them who believe and profess such things as seem unto them so agreeable to the Rule of Faith. But it would be very ill done to obtrude those things upon others, unto whom they do not seem to be the indubitable Doctrines of the Scripture. And to make a Separation for such things as these, which neither are nor can be fundamental, is to become Hereticks. For I do not think there is any man arrived to that degree of madness, as that he dare give out his Consequences and Interpretations of Scripture as Divine Inspirations, and compare the Articles of Faith that he has framed according to his own Fancy with the Authority of the Scripture. I know there are some Propositions so evidently agreeable to Scripture, that no body can deny them to be drawn from thence: but about those therefore there can be no difference. This only I say, that however clearly we may think this or the other Doctrine to be deduced from Scripture, we ought not therefore to impose it upon others, as a necessary Article of Faith, because we believe it to be agreeable to the Rule of Faith; unless we would be content also that other Doctrines should be imposed upon us in the same manner; and that we should be compell'd to receive and profess all the different and contradictory Opinions of *Lutherans, Calvinists, Remonstrants, Anabaptists,* and other Sects, which the Contrivers of Symbols, Systems and Confessions, are accustomed to deliver unto their Followers as genuine and necessary Deductions from the Holy Scripture. I cannot but wonder at the extravagant arrogance of those men who think that they themselves can explain things necessary to Salvation more clearly than the Holy Ghost, the Eternal and Infinite Wisdom of God.

Thus much concerning *Heresy;* which word in common use is applied only to the Doctrinal part of Religion. Let us now consider *Schism,* which is a Crime near a-kin to it. For both those words seem unto me to signifie an *ill-grounded Separation in Ecclesiastical Communion, made about things not necessary.* But since Use, which is the Supream Law in matter of Language, has determined that Heresy relates to Errors in Faith, and Schism to those in Worship or Discipline, we must consider them under that Distinction.

Schism then, for the same reasons that have already been alledged, is nothing else but a Separation made in the Communion of the Church, upon account of something in Divine Worship, or Ecclesiastical Discipline, that is not any necessary part of it. Now nothing in Worship or Discipline can be necessary to Christian Communion, but what Christ our Legislator, or the Apostles, by Inspiration of the Holy Spirit, have commanded in express words.

In a word: He that denies not any thing that the holy Scriptures teach in express words, nor makes a Separation upon occasion of any thing that is not manifestly contained in the Sacred Text; however he may be nick-named by any Sect of Christians, and declared by some, or all of them to be utterly void of true Christianity, yet indeed and in truth this man cannot be either a Heretick or Schismatick.

These things might have been explained more largely, and more advantageously: but it is enough to have hinted at them, thus briefly, to a Person of your parts.

FINIS.

Bibliography

Primary sources

Bagshawe, Edward. 1660. *The Great Question Concerning Things Indifferent in Religious Worship*. London.

Bagshawe, Edward. 1661. *The Second Part of the Great Question Concerning Things Indifferent in Religious Worship*. London.

Bunyan, John. 1966. *Grace Abounding to the Chief of Sinners and The Pilgrim's Progress from this world to that which is to Come*. Ed. and intro. by R. Sharrock. London, Oxford University Press.

Burnet, Gilbert. 1833. *History of his own Time*. 6 volumes. London: second edition.

Calamy, Edward. 1802. *The Non-Conformists' Memorial being an Account of the Ministers who were Ejected or Silenced after the Restoration*. 2 vols. London.

Filmer, Sir Robert. 1949. *Patriarcha and other Political Works of Sir Robert Filmer*. Ed. and intro. by Peter Laslett. Oxford, Basil Blackwell.

Locke, John. 1660–1662. *Two Tracts on Government*. Tr., ed. and intro. by Philip Abrams. Cambridge: Cambridge University Press, 1967.

Locke, John. 1667. *An Essay Concerning Toleration*. MS. Locke c.28 fol.21. Reprinted in Carlo Viano. 1961. John Locke. *Scritti Editi e Inediti Sulla Tolleranza*. Turino: Taylor.

Locke, John. 1675. *A Letter from a Person of Quality to his Friend in the Country*. London. In *Works* 1823. Vol. 10.

Locke, John. 1679. *Toleratio*. MS. Locke. d.1, p. 125–126. (Bodleian Library).

Locke, John and James Tyrrell. c. 1681. *Critical Notes on Edward Stillingfleet. The Mischief of Separation*. MS. Locke c.34 (Bodleian Library).

Locke, John. 1689. *Epistola de Tolerantia*. Gouda. In Montuori 1963.

Locke, John. 1689. *A Letter Concerning Toleration*. London.

Locke, John. 1690. *A Letter Concerning Toleration*. Second Edition. London.

Locke, John. 1689. *Two Treatises of Government*. London.

Locke, John. 1690. *The Second Letter Concering Toleration*. London. In *Works*. 1823. Vol. 6.

Locke, John. 1692. *A Third Letter for Toleration to the Author of the Third Letter Concerning Toleration*. London. In *Works*. 1823. Vol. 6.

Locke, John. 1695. *The Reasonableness of Christianity*. London. In *Works*. 1823. Vol. 7.

Locke, John. 1704. *A Fourth Letter for Toleration*. In *Works*. 1823. Vol. 6.

Locke, John. 1976. *The Correspondence of John Locke*. Ed. E.S. de Beer. 8 vols. Oxford: Clarendon Press, vol. 1.

Locke, John. 1823. *The Works of John Locke*. 10 vols. London.

Long, Thomas. 1689. *The Letter for Toleration decipher'd and the absurdity of an absolute Toleration demonstrated*. London.

Penn, William. 1726. *A Collection of the Works of William Penn*. 2 vols. London.

Proast, Jonas. 1690. *The Argument of the Letter Concerning Toleration Briefly Considered and Answered*. London.

Proast. Jonas. 1691. *The Third Letter Concerning Toleration*. London.

Proast, Jonas. 1703. *A Second Letter to the Author of the Three Letters for Toleration*. London.

Stillingfleet, Edward. 1680. *The Mischief of Separation*. London.

Stillingfleet, Edward. 1681. *The Unreasonableness of Separation*. London.

Stubbe, Henry. 1659. *An Essay in Defence of the Good Old Cause*. London.

Secondary sources

Abrams, Philip. 1967. Introduction. John Locke. *Two Tracts on Government*. Cambridge: Cambridge University Press.

America's Watch Committee and the American Civil Liberties Union. 1982. *Report on Human Rights in El Salvador*. New York: Random House.

Ashcraft, Richard. 1980. Revolutionary Politics and Locke's *Two Treatises of Government*. *Political Theory*. Vol. 8, 4 (November 1980), pp. 429–487.

Barnet, Richard. 1981. *The Lean Years. Politics in the Age of Scarcity*. New York: Simon and Schuster.

Berger, Thomas. 1982. *Fragile Freedoms. Human Rights and Dissent in Canada*. Toronto: Clark, Irwin and Company.

Bosher, Robert. 1951. *The Making of the Restoration Settlement. The Influence of the Laudians 1649–1662*. Oxford: Oxford University Press.

Chomsky, Noam and Edward Herman. 1979. *The Political Economy of Human Rights*. 2 vols. Montreal: Black Rose Books.

Cragg, G.R. 1950. *From Puritanism to the Age of Reason. A Study in the Changes in the Religious Thought within the Church of England 1660–1700*. Cambridge: Cambridge University Press.

Cragg, G.R. 1957. *Puritanism in the Period of the Great Persecution 1660–1688*. Cambridge: Cambridge University Press.

Cranston, Maurice. 1957. *John Locke: A Biography*. London Longman, Green.

Donner, Frank. 1981. *The Age of Surveillance. The Aims and Methods of America's Intelligence System*. New York: Vintage Books.

Dunn, John. 1969. *The Political Thought of John Locke*. Cambridge Cambridge University Press.

Dunn, John. 1983. *John Locke*. Oxford: Oxford University Press. Forthcoming.

Earle, Peter. 1977. *Monmouth's Rebels: The road to Sedgemoor 1685*. New York: St. Martin's Press.

Ebbinghaus, Julius von. 1957. Einleitung. John Locke. *Ein Brief über Toleranz*. Englisch-deutsch. Hamburg: Verlag von Felix Meiner.

Foucault, Michel. 1980. Lecture two: 14 January 1976. *Power/ Knowledge: Selected Interviews and other Writings 1972–1977*. Ed. Colin Gordon. New York: Pantheon Books, pp. 92–108.

Franklin, Julian. 1978. *John Locke and the Theory of Sovereignty*. Cambridge: Cambridge University Press.

Goldie, Mark. 1980. The Roots of True Whiggism, 1688–1694. *History of Political Thought*. Vol. 1, 2 (Summer, June 1980), pp. 195–236.

Goldie, Mark. 1983. John Locke and Anglican Royalism. *History of Political Thought. Political Studies* 31 (1983) 61–85.

Haley, K.D.H. 1968. *The First Earl of Shaftesbury*. Oxford: Oxford University Press.

Henriques, Ursula. 1961. *Religious Toleration in England 1787–1833*. London: Routledge and Kegan Paul.

Hundert, Edward. 1972. The Making of Homo-Faber: John Locke between Ideology and History. *Journal of the History of Ideas*. Vol. 33, 1, pp. 3–22.

Jacob, Margaret. 1981. *The Radical Enlightenment*. Ithaca: Cornell University Press.

Jones, J.R. 1978. *Country and Court. England 1658–1714*. London: Edward Arnold.

Jordan, W.K. 1940. *Development of Religious Toleration in England*. 4 vols. London: George Allen and Unwin (1932–1940).

Kamen, Henry. 1967. *The Rise of Toleration*. London: Weidenfeld and Nicolson.

Kraynak, Robert. 1980. John Locke: from Absolutism to Toleration. *American Political Science Review* 74 (March 1980), pp. 53–69.

Lacey, Douglas. 1969. *Dissent and Parliamentary Politics in England, 1661–1689*. New Brunswick: Rutgers University Press.

Laslett, Peter. 1970. Introduction. John Locke. *Two Treatises of Government*. Cambridge University Press.

Lecky, W.E.H. 1880. *The Rise and Influence of Rationalism in Europe*. 2 vols. London.

Lecler, Joseph. 1960. *Toleration and the Reformation*. Tr. T.L. Westow. 2 vols. New York.

Lernoux, Penny. 1982. *Cry of the People. The Struggle for Human Rights in Latin America. The Catholic Church in Conflict with U.S. Policy*. Middlesex: Penguin.

Miller, John. 1973. *Popery and Politics in England 1660–1688*. Cambridge: Cambridge University Press.

Montuorio, Mario. 1963. Introduction. John Locke. *A Letter Concerning Toleration*. Latin and English Texts. The Hague: Martinus Nijhoff.

Parry, Geraint. 1978. *John Locke*. London: George Allen and Unwin.
Passmore, J.A. 1978. *Locke and the Ethics of Belief*. Dawes Hicks Lecture on Philosophy, British Academy 1978. Oxford: Oxford University Press.
Popkin, Richard. 1979. *The History of Scepticism from Erasmus to Spinoza*. Berkeley: University of California Press.
Power, Jonathan. 1981. *Against Oblivion. Amnesty International's Fight for Human Rights*. London: Fontana.
Skinner, Quentin. 1978. *The Foundations of Modern Political Thought*. Volume 2: *The Reformation*. Cambridge: Cambridge University Press.
Stankiewicz, W.J. 1960. *Politics and Religion in Seventeenth Century France*. Berkeley: University of California Press.
Thompson, E.P. 1968. *The Making of the English Working Class*. 2nd edition. Middlesex: Penguin.
Thomas, Roger. 1962. *Comprehension and Indulgence*. Geoffrey Nuttall and Owen Chadwick (eds.) *From Uniformity to Unity*. London: S.P.C.K., pp. 189–255.
Tuck, Richard. 1979. *Natural Rights Theories. Their Origin and Development*. Cambridge: Cambridge University Press.
Van Leeuwen, Henry. 1963. *The Problem of Certainty in English Thought 1630–1690*. The Hague: Martinus Nijhoff.
Veliz, Claudio. 1981. *The Centralist Tradition of Latin America*. Princeton: Princeton University Press.
Viano, Carlo Augusto. 1960. *John Locke, dal Razionalismo all'Illuminismo*. Turin: Taylor.
Viano, Carlo Augusto. 1961. *John Locke, Scritti Editi e Inediti Sulla tolleranza*. Turin: Taylor.
Walker, D.P. 1964. *The Decline of Hell*. London: Routledge and Kegan Paul.
Watts, Michael. 1978. *The Dissenters from the Reformation to the French Revolution*. Oxford: Clarendon Press.
Weston, Caroline Comstock and J.R. Greenberg. 1981. *Subjects and Sovereigns. The Grand Controversy over Legal Sovereignty in Stuart England*. Cambridge: Cambridge University Press.
Wootton, David. 1983. *Atheism, Irreligion and the Social Order*. Cambridge: Cambridge University Press. Forthcoming.
Yolton, John. 1957. *John Locke and the Way of Ideas*. Oxford: Oxford University Press.